The Wonder Within You

HAROLD KLEMP

ECKANKAR
Minneapolis
Eckankar.org

The Wonder within You

 220607

Printed in USA

Compiled by Crary Brouhard and Shelley Hyndman
Illustrations by Crary Brouhard and Raoof Haghighi

Library of Congress Cataloging-in-Publication Data

Names: Klemp, Harold, author.

Title: The wonder within you / Harold Klemp.

Description: 1st. | Minneapolis : Eckankar, [2022] | Audience: Ages 13-17 | Audience: Grades 7-9 | Summary: "Author Harold Klemp, spiritual leader of Eckankar, shares with youth the unique Spiritual Exercises of ECK, which can revitalize a person in every way imaginable. A true gift from God that will open the heart to new adventure, helping one build a happy life, solve problems, and find comfort and peace" -- Provided by publisher.

Identifiers: LCCN 2022034379 | ISBN 9781570435348 (paperback)

Subjects: LCSH: Eckankar (Organization)--Doctrines. | Spiritual life--Eckankar (Organization)

Classification: LCC BP605.E3 K583 2022 | DDC 299/.93--dc23/eng/20220723

LC record available at https://lccn.loc.gov/2022034379

♾ This paper meets the requirements of ANSI/NISO Z39.48-1992 (Permanence of Paper).

Sri Doug Kunin
The MAHANTA,
the Living ECK Master

Historic Event

At the 2025 ECK Worldwide Soul Adventure Seminar, Harold Klemp announced Sri Doug Kunin as his successor, the new MAHANTA, the Living ECK Master.

Sri Doug began his term as the spiritual leader of ECKANKAR on October 22, 2025.

The last occasion of succession occurred October 22, 1981, when Harold Klemp began his term as the spiritual leader of ECKANKAR.

The change in spiritual leadership is always a step forward for the consciousness of the worlds. The role of the Living ECK Master has always been to awaken the love for the divine things already within the human heart.

ECKANKAR
The Path of Spiritual Freedom
Eckankar.org

Table of Contents

CREATE YOUR WORLD

DISCOVER YOURSELF AS SOUL

DREAM WISDOM

ECK MASTERS AND YOU

EXPLORE THE GOD WORLDS OF ECK

INNER GUIDANCE

LIGHT-AND-SOUND-OF-GOD ADVENTURES

MEET THE MAHANTA

PAST LIVES, PRESENT LESSONS

PROBLEM SOLVING

PROTECTION

SOUL TRAVEL AND DIVINE IMAGINATION

THE WONDERS OF SERVICE TO LIFE

Sri Harold Klemp,
the MAHANTA, the Living ECK Master

Welcome

Dear One,

You are holding a golden key. It is one of a kind—unlike anyone else's. And it perfectly fits the door to the wonder within *you*.

What is this golden key?

It's your own practice of the Spiritual Exercises of ECK. You will have experiences no one else has ever had. These experiences come from the bond of love between you and the MAHANTA, the Inner Master.

It's a very real love. A love as much a part of you as your own heartbeat.

The wonder within you is also a very real treasure. It is the source of all your confidence, happiness, strength, love, and creativity. You are Soul, an atom of God. Earth is a school to learn all about being an atom of God. There are other schools too, which we can visit in your contemplations and dreams.

Everything that happens to you in life is to help you become an ECK Master—a Coworker with God.

Your spiritual exercises bring you awareness and inner guidance, help you solve your own problems, give you comfort and peace, and open wide the doors to Soul adventures on earth and in the inner worlds.

Wonder indeed!

The Inner Master will be with you during every spiritual exercise you do, helping you explore and grow every day and night. But don't forget—you hold the key. Experiment with the ECK Spiritual Exercises, and make them your own. They are a gift from God.

The doors of HU are ready to open for you! See page 9.

With love and blessings,

Harold

About the Spiritual Exercises of ECK

Each of us is Soul, a unique spark of God on a journey to

- discover who we truly are,
- learn how to give and receive divine love, and
- return home to the heart of God.

That's what the school of life and the Spiritual Exercises of ECK are all about.

Discover who you truly are.

Build Your Inner Strength

Spiritual exercises are a lot like physical exercises. When we do physical exercises, we use our physical muscles and build strength in our body. In a spiritual exercise, you, as Soul, use your inner faculties and build spiritual strength to meet life and fulfill your highest potential.

Why Do the Spiritual Exercises?

The spiritual exercises give you confidence in yourself as Soul. You can meet the Inner Master, the MAHANTA, who is a friend and guide on your journey. And you can see the Light and hear the Sound of God.

Together, the Light and Sound are the Voice of God. They are God's love for you. Experience with these two aspects of God is the whole focus of the ECK teachings. The Light shows us the path before us, and the Sound leads us home.

"Am I Doing Them Right?"

Often people ask if they are doing the exercises correctly. There is no one right way to do the spiritual exercises! Each of us is different. Some people have quite an active inner life and travel widely in the inner worlds; others simply let Divine Spirit guide them indirectly in their daily lives. So fit the exercises in this book to you. The Inner Master will help you with this.

There is no one right way to do the spiritual exercises.

Experiment with them, and see what works for you. If you eat the same food every day for two weeks, it can get pretty dull. You might enjoy it the first day, and the second day is all right. But by the second week, you're tired of it. It's the same with the spiritual exercises. So you experiment; you try new things. That's what I did. I have gone to different extremes with the exercises, trying very complicated ones I developed for myself, then dropping them when they didn't work anymore.

It's like a vein of gold running through a

mountain. You're on it for a while, then the vein runs out and you have to scout around and find another one.

Don't push yourself, though. There's no reason to push. Just relax and have fun as you explore your inner worlds and discover what it means to live from the perspective of Soul!

The most important thing is to fill yourself with love as you do this. It may help to think about someone or something you really love and let that love fill your heart. As you send that love back home to SUGMAD, or God, It sends much more love to you. It may feel like a warm blanket of Light and a gentle Sound all around you.

Fill yourself with love.

You are in your own God Worlds!

"What Should I Expect?"

This is another good question. Some people misunderstand the Spiritual Exercises of ECK because they look so simple. Some are disappointed that they are not getting certain results. What they do not realize is that the spiritual exercises are working at a higher level than their everyday awareness. The exercises work to tone and strengthen the spiritual muscles of Soul. At the same time, they are purifying the lower bodies. Those who patiently do the spiritual exercises out of love for God or the Master will find both their awareness and their creativity beginning to grow.

Most of the time, your experiences might be very subtle and therefore easy to miss. But occasionally they can also make you sit up and take notice, as if to remind you what is really happening when you do the spiritual exercises.

Ask yourself, Am I learning something new every day from what I'm doing? Am I getting insight, inner help, and guidance? This is what we are working for.

Ask yourself, Am I learning something new? Am I getting insight, inner help, and guidance?

So, let's get started. Just choose any of the spiritual exercises in this book that lights up for you, and give it a try.

You may want to try a new spiritual exercise every time, or you might choose an exercise that fits your specific interests or needs right now. Another option is to read one of the contemplation seeds given at the beginning of each chapter; just take the short passage into contemplation, and see what new insight or awareness the ECK brings you.

You can also use the special journal pages at the end of each chapter, either to record your adventures, experiences, and spiritual discoveries or to make note of your favorite spiritual exercises—ones you want to try again in the future.

Have fun!

ACCEPTING

DIVINE LOVE

Contemplation Seeds

You exist because God loves you.

HU is a carrier of love
between God and Soul.

People often wonder, *How do I get God's love?* You get it by giving of yourself to others, in ways that you like to give.

Begin with the love you have.
This love expands your heart
into a greater vessel
which can hold yet more love.

On the outside, divine and emotional love may look the same, but divine love is joyful, thankful. It gives itself fully.

Doors of HU

In contemplation, visualize two front doors of the Temple of ECK in Chanhassen, Minnesota. On the left door see a big golden *H* and on the right door a big golden *U.*

God loves you immensely.

Sing *HU* as you walk to the doors, open them, and enter the Temple.

The MAHANTA, the Living ECK Master is waiting for you inside. He greets you and has something special to share with you, something that will help you grow spiritually. It might be a bit of wisdom, an insight into life, or a heart-opening message just for you. Whatever it is, it tells of God's immense love for you.

What does the Master show you?

Take a moment to fully accept this gift of love with your entire heart. It can change your life.

A Wonderland of Love

Whenever you want to feel God's love for you, try this spiritual exercise at bedtime.

Close your eyes as you prepare to go to sleep. Far off in the distance, look for a dot of golden light. It will be dim at first, then it will get bigger and brighter as it moves quickly toward you.

The Light and Sound of God is your key.

Watch it grow in size until you clearly see it is the EK symbol—the letters *EK.*

Concentrate on the golden EK, and softly chant *HU,* the sacred name of God. Soon you will see the Light and hear the Sound of God. This Light and Sound of God is your key to the wonderland of God's divine love for you. Soak in the love, and go explore this new land.

What do you discover there?

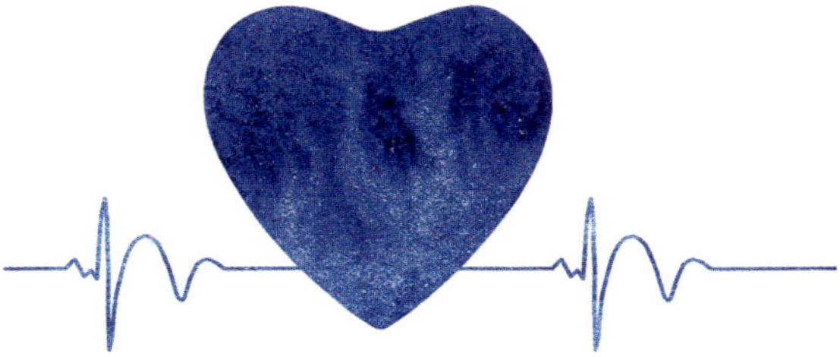

Breathing In the Mahanta's Love

Let your heartbeat remind you of the Mahanta's love.

Find a comfortable place to lie down, and place a drawing or picture of the Living ECK Master over your chest where your heart is.

Gently chant *Wah Z*. Pay attention to the rhythm of your breathing and your heartbeat. Imagine that with every breath you take you are opening yourself a little more to your love for the Mahanta and the Mahanta's love for you.

Every beat of your heart reminds you that this love is always with you, flowing into every part of your life.

Collecting Joy

One way to fill yourself with love is by remembering someone or something that has brought you great happiness. Who do you love? What do you love?

Feel the love you have for this person or this experience. Let it pour out from your heart and fill every part of your being.

Sprinkle happiness on your present and future.

Now imagine yourself above time, where you can see your whole life—past, present, and future. See all the truly happy moments from your life up to now, and picture them as waves rolling up onto a beach. Then collect some of that joy, go forward in time, and sprinkle this water of happiness on your present and future.

Leave it there for Divine Spirit to bring you Its gifts of happiness and love, both now and in years to come.

Tip: If you want to keep the blessings of life coming to you, be grateful for what you have and for whatever is given. This gratitude will begin to create a series of events all for your spiritual benefit.

Count Your Blessings

Do you want to be more open to love and joy? There is a special technique that can help bring this about.

Unlike other spiritual exercises, it does not have a beginning, middle, and end. This technique involves attitude, and it is one that must be lived. In a word, it's called *gratitude.*

Throughout the day contemplate on all the blessings in your life. Choose a time every day to write down or focus on at least three things in your life that you are sincerely grateful for.

The power of gratitude opens the heart.

You can practice gratitude for the gift of life itself and for your own body, mind, and emotions. For all the small things that help you exist in this world and help you unfold and gain experience.

Saying, "Thank you," aloud or in your heart, is a way to feel God's love.

When you practice gratitude in this way,

you may find that you take extra care with your food and physical well-being, or that you are kinder to yourself and others.

The power of gratitude opens the heart to allow love to enter. Once the love comes in, and we receive the gifts of Divine Spirit and of life, the way to keep the gifts flowing is to be grateful.

Healing Heartache

If you are experiencing heartache or loneliness, here is a spiritual exercise to try. Read the exercise over twice before you begin. Each time you try it, you will experience an inner healing of divine love, and the hurt may feel less.

Close your eyes, and imagine a beautiful, red-and-white, ceramic heart that is broken in half. Notice that there is a tube of glue next to the heart. The label on the tube reads "Mahanta's Love."

Open the tube, and apply glue to the broken edges of the heart. As you put the pieces together, you notice they fit so well it is hard to see where the heart was ever broken.

Feel loved, refreshed, and at peace.

Pick up the healed heart, and hold it to your chest. Notice it is warm and now glows with a soft, golden light. Hold this golden heart as long as you wish, and welcome its warmth. Feel your own heart glowing with the Mahanta's love.

When you open your eyes, you feel loved, refreshed, and at peace. How will you express gratitude for this love?

Worthy of God's Love

This spiritual exercise is about knowing you are worthy of God's love.

Sit in a comfortable position, and chant your secret word or one of the spiritually charged words of ECK, such as *SUGMAD*, *HU*, or *Wah Z*.

Receive a gift of divine love.

Do this until you feel you are floating in soft sound. Say to yourself, "I am worthy of the SUGMAD's love." Repeat it a few times.

Now imagine the MAHANTA giving you a gift of divine love. What is it?

Wah Z will spend some time with you, showing you how to make use of this gift for your own happiness and for the happiness of others. How will you put it to good use?

Gratitude for Your Body

Open your heart, and sing *Alayi*, the word for the physical plane, for several minutes.

As you sing, listen to this beautiful sound. Let it remind you of all the things you are grateful for about having a physical body and the many spiritual opportunities this brings you.

See your body as a sacred temple for Soul to experience life in this physical world.

Your body is a sacred temple.

Make a list of everything you are grateful for about your physical body, and read it over at bedtime. Ask the Inner Master to show you how your body is a gift to you in this lifetime.

What do you learn?

Loving yourself is a key step to spiritual freedom.

The Eternal Nature of Soul

Enjoy this feeling of limitlessness.

Chant *HU* for several minutes. Then imagine yourself, Soul, as a body of golden light. God's love for you pulses in the center of the light. Let this love and light expand until you have no beginning or ending. Enjoy this feeling of limitlessness.

Ask the Inner Master to give you a glimpse of the boundless love and creativity of who you truly are—Soul. What do you see?

Journal Your Experience

Write or draw anything you see, feel, hear, or experience during your spiritual exercise.

Journal Your Experience

Write or draw anything you see, feel, hear, or experience during your spiritual exercise.

BALANCE AND

HARMONY

Contemplation Seeds

Love tries to find a harmonious
way to resolve a situation.

Problems of one sort or another
are always with us in some form.
They are to make us strong.

Learn to treat yourself gently.

You are the star in your own world.

A Majestic Eagle

This is a very easy spiritual exercise to help you rise above the blind emotions that get stirred up by the challenges of daily life.

See yourself as a majestic eagle. Imagine soaring far above the physical world. Catch the wind beneath your wings, and feel it ruffling your feathers. Soar upward. Watch the earth and the rainy clouds that cover it fall away far, far beneath you. Feel the fresh air. See the crystal-blue sky around you.

Rise above the emotions and challenges of life.

As you soar, chant one of the special words of ECK: *HU*, *Sugmad*, or *Wah Z*, the spiritual name of the Living ECK Master. Or chant your own secret word if you have one.

Now look up. There is the sun! In its surprisingly soft light stands the Mahanta. Listen carefully. In some way he will share what it means to be an eagle in ECK and how you can begin to live in that state. Afterward, remember to write down what he says!

Anger or Control?

To get in control of your anger, try to catch yourself when you're in the middle of an argument with someone. Then chant *HU*, the holy name for God, softly to yourself. Take a step back, as Soul, and let the argument run its natural course, just to see what it does to your emotions.

Self-control is freedom.

Suddenly you may be surprised to find you are now in control of whether to argue or not, instead of being a helpless victim of your mind. Try this, and see how it works.

You can even try a version of this exercise after you've had an argument. Replay it in your mind, and ask the MAHANTA, "How could I have handled this without anger?"

Self-control is freedom. See how it works for you.

How Is My Balance?

This spiritual exercise can bring a new kind of balance to your life if you do it several days in a row.

Sit quietly, and picture yourself at a beach. You can hear the ocean waves crashing on the shore, and the clean sand feels good when you let it run through your bare toes. Beside you is the MAHANTA. He is holding a scale which has two shallow bowls for weighing things. Ask him, "How is my balance?" Ask about your physical body one day, then about another body—your emotional, memory, mind, or Soul body—on other days.

The MAHANTA will put golden sand in the scale bowls to show your state of balance for the area of your life that you asked about that day. If something looks out of balance, ask, "What can I do to balance this area and align it with the ECK?" Listen for his suggestion, and try it during the day. You may get an inner reminder from the Master.

Put positive energy into everything you do.

When you are in balance, there will be more positive energy in everything you do!

Balancing Soul's Five Bodies

Close your eyes and picture a room with six comfortable chairs. Imagine the MAHANTA coming into the room and sitting in one of the chairs. You—as Soul—take one chair and invite your Physical, Astral, Causal, and Mental bodies to take the remaining four chairs. Each body is dressed in a color that represents the plane it works on: the Physical body in green, the Astral in pink, the Causal in orange, and the Mental in blue.

Listen from the viewpoint of Soul.

With the MAHANTA's help, ask each body what it needs in order to be completely healthy and happy. Let your most active body speak first. Listen from the viewpoint of Soul as each body tells you what it needs.

Now turn to the MAHANTA and ask his advice. How can you help each body get the nourishment it needs? Be sure to write your insights from this exercise in your journal.

What is your next step?

The Fan Technique

Sometimes we develop unhealthy habits. If you have a habit you'd like to release, ask the MAHANTA for help.

Heal bad habits.

Imagine yourself living free from the habit. Visualize your body as a temple—clean, clear, and healthy. You feel lighter and full of fresh energy.

In contemplation, chant the word for detachment, which is *vairag* (vie-RAHG). Imagine standing with the MAHANTA in front of a huge fan. The air from the fan is gently flowing over your body. As you chant *vairag*, feel layers of karma being blown away from you by the gentle currents. Stand in front of the fan as long as you'd like.

Everything that is taken away is replaced with freedom and love.

Tip: Watch and listen for the MAHANTA's guidance as he continues to help you make the change you desire.

Perfect Balance

Sing *HU* for a few minutes, and feel the presence of the MAHANTA within you.

With your Spiritual Eye, see a large golden EK symbol. You are standing with the Master, perfectly balanced at the very top of the rounded EK. A gentle wind is blowing. Notice how naturally you lean or shift to stay balanced as the wind swirls around you. What guidance does the Master give to help you maintain your balance?

Feel the presence of the MAHANTA within you.

Imagine that feeling of perfect balance filling your inner bodies. Take five to ten minutes for this exercise. It can help you build strength to deal with karma.

Watch your daily life for signs that you are learning more about balance. You may have dreams about balance—such as walking a tightrope, ice skating or skiing, or juggling. Record these dreams in your dream journal, because they are examples of balance in your inner and outer life.

In your day, this experience of balance may change you. It can be as simple as softening an opinion, going out of your way for someone, or not reacting to a problem.

Recharge Your Spiritual Strength

The word *HU* has a unique ability to lift you into a higher state of awareness. It can recharge you spiritually.

You know how you plug a device in to charge the battery when it runs low? Well, similarly, you can plug yourself into the HU and charge yourself spiritually.

Sing *HU* for a few minutes, and imagine entering a Temple of Golden Wisdom. The MAHANTA greets you at the door and leads you to a room where the HU is playing. Make yourself comfortable, and listen. Feel free to sing along with your own sound of HU. Feel Its power charge your spiritual bodies with love, energy, health, and wisdom.

You have the love of HU inside you.

Stay for as long as you like. When you are ready, open your eyes, and go about your day knowing you have the sound and love of the HU inside you every moment.

Blessings for Balance

If you are holding negative attitudes about people, how can you let go and feel the love of the MAHANTA? Here are three ways:

1. If you meet someone you have negative feelings about, silently say to yourself, "In the name of the SUGMAD." Repeat this phrase to yourself each time this occurs, blessing the situation and letting it go.
2. Be polite when these people are near you, and chant *HU* silently within yourself. Listen to the person while you chant, rather than getting into a long conversation with them. Say as little as possible while still remaining polite.
3. In your imagination, see the MAHANTA near you.

Release negative attitudes.

When you bless a situation, you keep yourself in balance and do not become involved in negative conditions. This way you can be a true channel for the ECK, and miracles can take place.

The Freedom Bridge

Regain your balance.

If you'd like to regain balance, imagine you are walking with the MAHANTA across a long, beautiful bridge in the inner worlds. What do you see below? Maybe birds flying underneath, or mountains far away. Look around!

When you reach the middle of the bridge, notice that you feel a great freedom and joy. All is balanced in your world at this very moment. The Master's eyes shine with love for you, and your heart smiles deep inside.

During the day, whenever you need, remember this special experience of love and balance with Wah Z. He remembers too.

Journal Your Experience

Write or draw anything you see, feel, hear, or experience during your spiritual exercise.

Journal Your Experience

Write or draw anything you see, feel, hear, or experience during your spiritual exercise.

CREATE

YOUR WORLD

Contemplation Seeds

If you can dream something,
you can do it.

If there is something you want in life, do everything within your power to bring it about. When you haven't the power to do any more, Divine Spirit will help you in some way.

You are the creator in your own worlds, whether they are on the inner planes or out here in the physical.

If you can achieve an improvement over yesterday, even if it's small, you have gained significantly. You are taking charge of your own world. You are becoming a creator.

A Way to Build Self-Confidence

If you lack self-confidence, use this technique to build yourself up again.

First find the spots in your aura, or within yourself, that are self-conscious, shy, timid, or overly sensitive. These tend to attract people who take advantage of your weakness. Inwardly, ask those people to move out of your way. Mentally demand respectful attention.

Next identify and focus on the opposite qualities of mind and character to replace those self-conscious qualities. Fill yourself with the positive quality of courage so that the positive force you create can actually be felt when you pass through a room.

Be direct and positive in your approach.

Adopt the mental attitude and personal bearing of a person with great confidence. Always be direct and positive in your approach to all things. Put all your spiritual force behind your smile, your replies, and your thoughts.

Practice this daily, and ask the MAHANTA to help you make this inner change.

The Contract Technique

Lay the groundwork for success.

The Contract technique gives you a creative way to complete things and practice self-discipline.

Since the MAHANTA is always interested in helping us discover new spiritual abilities and awareness, we can make a contract with him to get important things done in our lives and still have plenty of time to enjoy life.

For example, make a contract with the MAHANTA to get your homework done. You might say, “I will study for my math exam from 10:00 a.m. to 11:00 a.m. on Saturday. I will put all my energy into it and do it as well as I can. Then I can go to the baseball game with my friends.” Since it is your special contract, put in any details you want.

Setting a specific time for doing important things is like making a date with the MAHANTA. It helps you follow through with your plans. It also reminds you that you are not alone.

It not only makes the work easier, but you will find that the energy you reserved for time with your friends will also be there.

What would you like to focus on and get done? You can make a contract with the MAHANTA during your spiritual exercise. Then be sure to write it down in your journal. See how this works for you.

Tip: The best contract you can make is to do the Spiritual Exercises of ECK each day. This lays the groundwork for all success!

A Little Box of ECK

To help you replace negative thoughts during hard times, try this idea suggested by an ECK youth. Make an "ECK box." Cut a sheet of paper into about twenty-four pieces; on each slip of paper, write a different ECK principle, loving thought, or light-hearted idea.

Here are some examples:

"Soul is a happy, creative being."

"I love you."

"Let the MAHANTA guide you."

Replace negative thoughts.

"Don't let the negative power interfere with your life."

Place the pieces of paper into your box. Whenever you feel mad or sad, pull out a piece of paper and read it aloud.

These small ECK reminders will help chase negative thoughts away. They can lighten up the darker attitudes that slip into our consciousness now and then.

Create a Brighter World

If you have an uncomfortable experience or one you don't understand, take it into contemplation.

Begin by singing *HU* for a few minutes. Then run the experience through your mind. Next, visualize a door that opens into golden sunlight. This is the Light of God.

Take charge of your life.

Now take the uncomfortable experience through the open doorway into golden sunlight. Watch it dissolve in the Light and Sound of God.

You may not feel anything change right away, but trust that the Light and Sound of God are at work. Practice this exercise every day until you feel a shift in your feelings or gain an understanding of the experience. Sometimes it can take a little while before we are able to see the gift or lesson that the experience offers.

This exercise can get you in the habit of looking for a brighter, more creative world.

With the help of the Inner Master, the MAHANTA, you are learning to take charge of your life.

You are becoming the aware Soul, the creator of your own worlds.

The Golden Parachute

If you are facing a new experience and feel nervous, anxious, or unsure about it, sing *HU* for a few minutes.

During your contemplation, look at the situation from above, from the Soul perspective. Imagine yourself gently floating down into the situation using a golden parachute. The parachute is being guided by the MAHANTA and is carrying you safely into the situation with love and grace.

Embrace change.

With the MAHANTA by your side, imagine yourself learning whatever you need to learn and doing whatever you need to do.

Freedom through Vairag

In contemplation, sing the word *vairag* (vie-RAHG) in a gentle whisper. This is a spiritual word that means detachment, a quality all ECK Masters have.

With each breath, see yourself, Soul, rising a little higher like a balloon filling with warm air. Imagine letting go of anything that no longer serves your highest goals. As you float along, watch your attachments or unhealthy habits fall away from you and into the ocean below. Watch them dissolve in the waves of the sea.

You may suddenly find yourself in an experience of the Light and Sound. What do you see? What do you hear?

Rise higher.

Ask the Inner Master to show you how to exercise this new sense of freedom in your inner and outer life. It may be as simple as having more patience or a greater sense of humor, or feeling more neutral about something that previously bothered you.

Overcoming Procrastination

When you are having trouble getting started on a project, try this spiritual exercise to understand the real purpose of what needs to be done.

For example, does studying math give you a better grasp of how the world of finance works? Does studying grammar give you the skills to better communicate what you think and feel? Does tidying your room help you find the items you need when you need them? What is the gift to you?

Find the energy to get started.

In contemplation, ask the MAHANTA to show you the deeper reason for each task you find yourself reluctant to begin. Knowing how something will benefit you may give you the energy to get started.

Goal-Setting Tests

Is there something you want in your life? Or a problem you'd like to deal with? Setting clear goals can help.

First, sing *HU* to spiritualize your consciousness and help you get the highest view possible at this time.

Second, your goals must pass four tests. Ask yourself the following questions: (1) Are my goals specific? (2) Are they realistic? (3) Can the outcome be clearly seen and verified? and (4) Have I given a date for completion? Write your goals down, making sure the answer to all these questions is yes.

Love is the true creative force.

Next, of course, you must begin working toward your goals in your daily life. Ask the Inner Master for guidance on the first step to take, and build from there. As you do this, you can also use visualization or daydreaming to help you. First picture the goal clearly—what you want to do or be in life. Then fill the picture with unbounded love, because love is the true creative force that removes all limitations.

Then keep taking each step toward your goal.

Practically all famous or successful people in the world have done this. The ECK Masters have set the goal of God-Realization and becoming a Coworker with God for the chela of ECK. Remembering this with love can pull you through rough times.

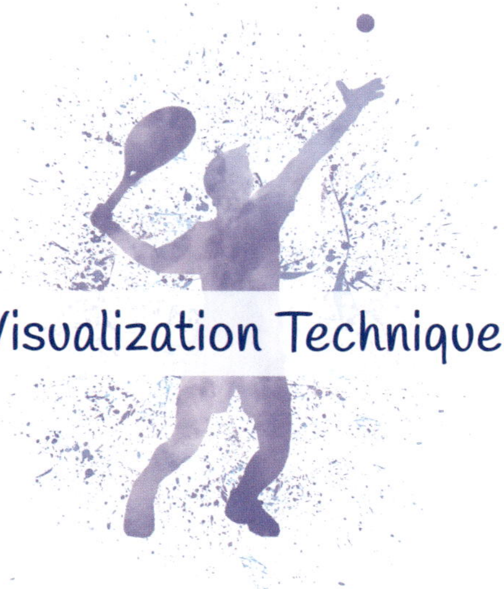

Visualization Technique

If you have difficulty visualizing on the inner, practice your visualization on something in your everyday life.

For example, if you like tennis, visualize (see) yourself playing a game of tennis after you go to bed at night. Practice your serve. Choose a place in your opponent's court where you want your serve to fall. Practice your serves in your imagination for five or ten minutes or until you fall asleep.

Discover the secret of creating a happier life.

Place your attention on the tennis ball instead of yourself. That draws your attention outward.

If you like some other activity more, like art, dancing, music, or basketball, then practice that in your imagination before going to sleep at night.

This technique will help you reach your everyday goals. How? You can start to regularly practice visualizing a goal you'd like to achieve, just as you visualized the activity you enjoy. Inwardly practice each step you need to take to accomplish your goal. What will you do?

With daily practice, you will find it easier and more natural to set and achieve your goals by using visualization and then outwardly taking the steps you visualized. You will then discover the secret of creating a happier, more successful life, because you, Soul, will have gained greater control over your thoughts, actions, dreams, and desires.

Thinking from the End

Thinking from the end means acting as if the goal you want is already yours. Think of a special goal to set for yourself. Something to help you move forward in the best direction. You can ask the Inner Master for guidance on what goal to set.

Practice the feeling of your goal fulfilled.

Then, in contemplation, *imagine* in every possible detail what it would feel like if you already achieved your goal. Practice seeing it, hearing it, touching it, and fully experiencing it in your imagination. Let yourself feel the joy of success right now. Each day, for one week, practice this feeling of your goal fulfilled. Allow it to build, and see what happens!

Thinking from the end can also be a technique for Soul Travel. For example, if you want to go to the Soul Plane, you can imagine what it looks like, what sounds you'll hear, and what you'll learn when you get there. Let yourself enjoy these things even before you think you've done them.

The secret of this approach is that it collapses time. In other words, it makes things happen more quickly—even instantly. You might suddenly realize that what you thought was your imagination was perfectly real all along!

Journal Your Experience

Write or draw anything you see, feel, hear, or experience during your spiritual exercise.

Journal Your Experience

Write or draw anything you see, feel, hear, or experience during your spiritual exercise.

Journal Your Experience

Write or draw anything you see, feel, hear, or experience during your spiritual exercise.

DISCOVER

YOURSELF AS SOUL

Contemplation Seeds

You exist because God loves you,
and that's all the reason
there needs to be. You are
important because you exist.

You are Soul. You are made
in the image of God. And
being made in the image of God,
you share the attributes of God—
freedom, power, and divine love.

Your spiritual destiny is to
grow in grace, love, and wisdom
until you can take your place
among the ECK Masters.

You're handmade in heaven, by
the Maker of life, love, freedom,
and happiness too. Be happy, be you,
just BE!

To Hear the Music of Soul

When you want to align your mind and body with your true voice, your true nature, your true heart, and just be Soul, try this spiritual exercise.

Find a quiet and peaceful place where you can relax and go within. Close your eyes, and take a few deep breaths. Begin to softly sing *HU* out loud.

After a few moments, you may start to hear a subtle, high sound like the ringing of a bell or the sweet song of wind chimes far away. When you think you can hear this sound, switch to singing *HU* silently so you can listen more closely.

The song of HU is part of you.

At first you may think it is only the sound of the air moving, but you are actually hearing the music of Soul—a sacred song of HU. It is a part of you. It is there in your voice whenever you speak with love.

Listen for this during your day.

A Look in the Mirror

With your Spiritual Eye, see yourself at the bank of a beautiful, rippling river in the company of the MAHANTA.

See your divine nature.

Watch as he reaches into the water and pulls out a shining mirror. Light dances from its surface. The Master holds it before you, and in it you see the true reflection of your divine nature, Soul.

What do you see? Contemplate on what this experience is showing you spiritually.

After you contemplate, you can draw or paint what you saw. More details may be revealed!

Beyond Limitations

The Shariyat-Ki-Sugmad, Book Two, says, on page 86, "One of the three truths of ECK is that Soul is immortal, and Its future is the future of a thing whose growth and splendor has no limits."

When you are facing a limitation in your inner or outer life, close your eyes and sing, "May the blessings be" for several minutes. Imagine hidden blessings of Light and Sound are raining into your life from the Ocean of Love and Mercy.

Take the next step.

Your acceptance of these blessings invites new possibilities. Look for how the ECK will lead you forward, and be ready and eager to take the next step when it is shown.

See the Godlike Qualities of Soul

As Soul, you have the same godlike qualities as the Living ECK Master. They are growing within you. The Inner Master helps you develop them so someday you can become an ECK Master.

You can become an ECK Master!

In contemplation, imagine the MAHANTA is standing before a whiteboard, ready to show you your own godlike qualities.

He may list them or replay a scene from your life to show you a particular quality in action. He will help you become aware of what godlike qualities you are developing today.

What qualities does the MAHANTA show you?

Using your inner guidance, choose one quality to focus on in your daily life over the next month or so. Watch to see how this special focus affects you and others in your life.

The Mental Fast

The mental fast is a sure way to burn off karma and grow spiritually. It will change you from the inside out.

This exercise can be done every Friday. Doing a mental fast means keeping your attention on the MAHANTA all day long. There are several ways to do it. One way is to sing *HU* inwardly or outwardly. Another way is to chant your secret word. Still another is to do everything that day in the name of the MAHANTA.

Change from the inside out.

You can keep your attention on the Inner Master as much as you can, or you can consciously remove every negative thought that comes up. Visualize it being put directly into the ECK Life Stream, where the Light and Sound of God can neutralize it. The mental fast can be done by anyone for their spiritual growth.

The key is to keep your attention on the highest.

Practice the Five Virtues

Develop your spiritual intelligence as Soul.

Practicing the five virtues of ECK—discrimination, forgiveness and tolerance, contentment, detachment, and humility—is a way to develop the spiritual intelligence of Soul. These virtues protect you from the snares of maya, or illusion. Each virtue counteracts one of the five passions of the mind—lust, anger, greed, attachment, and vanity. These mental passions are what cause our karma.

Pick a different virtue for each day or week, or even pick one for the whole month—whatever you wish.

Take a colorful sheet of paper. Write down the virtue you have selected. Write a definition of the virtue in your own words. Then put the paper on your bedroom wall or wherever you are likely to see it.

At night, sing *HU*, and imagine yourself

practicing your virtue. In contemplation, imagine the virtue as a shield of Light around your heart, or see yourself drinking from the cup of contentment, detachment, or whichever virtue you're working on. The Inner Master will help you create the experience that's right for you.

Practice the virtue as you go about your day.

After a month, discuss the five virtues with your parents and share what changes have come into your life.

The ECK Way to Pray

There are a lot of people who pray to God to get others to do things their way. They're using prayer to control others and bring about their own wishes. It's like a basketball team praying together before a game: "Dear God, help us win." Meanwhile, on the opposite side of the court the other guys are busy doing the same thing. What kind of prayer is that?

When you ask God for help, you can say, "Here's my problem, and I'd like your help in whatever way you see fit." We trust the wisdom of God, of the ECK, and of the MAHANTA.

Trust the wisdom of God.

This is the attitude of the ECKist. You look to see what you, yourself, can do to make things work; how you can overcome your own problem. And when you've done all you can, the ECK can take everything another step. It can work miracles if needed!

When you practice this, you are learning, unfolding, and getting experience to become a mature Soul—someone fit to be a Coworker with God.

Journal Your Experience

Write or draw anything you see, feel, hear, or experience during your spiritual exercise.

Journal Your Experience

Write or draw anything you see, feel, hear, or experience during your spiritual exercise.

DREAM

WISDOM

Contemplation Seeds

Dreams are a window to heaven. They link the two realities of heaven and earth—and allow you, as Soul, to move freely between them every single day when going to sleep.

Dreams touch every level of our life.
They may let us glimpse the future,
or give suggestions for healing,
or share insights into our relationships.

A spiritual dream is any dream. There is a spiritual side to every experience or event, no matter how large or small, and whether or not it occurs in everyday life or in a dream.

If the meaning of a certain dream is important for you spiritually, the Dream Master will send the message again and again through other dreams until you do get its meaning.
So relax and enjoy the ride.

A Way to Remember Your Dreams

If you don't dream, but you want to, this spiritual exercise is for you! The exercise is so simple that it may seem if I'm belittling your intelligence, but I'm not. Truth is always simple.

Just before you go to sleep, sit quietly on your bed. Close your eyes. Chant *HU* very softly, or if someone is in the room with you, chant It silently to yourself. HU is a special word, the ancient name for God. It has a power of Its own.

Make a commitment with Divine Spirit.

As you take the time to sit and chant *HU*, you are making a commitment with Divine Spirit.

Chant *HU* in a long, drawn-out way for three to five minutes, and let yourself settle down. Then wait for a few more minutes before starting the next step.

If you are unable to remember your dreams, simply chant the word *dream* spelled out. Chant it out loud, letter by letter: D-R-E-A-M. Do this for about five minutes.

Next, chant the same thing quietly for a few minutes, and then just go to sleep. As you are falling asleep, say, "I would like to remember an important spiritual dream." With this method, you are asking for truth to come through the dream state.

HU
A Healing Word

There is a way for you to get relief from nightmares, but it may not work overnight. It could take days or weeks if the problem has occurred over a period of years or stems from past lives.

Just before going to sleep, chant or sing *HU*, a name for God and a very healing word. Just sing, "HU-U-U-U" several times. As you do this, feel yourself filling with feelings of love, and then go to sleep. In a manner of speaking, as you chant *HU*, the lights go on inside you.

Get relief from nightmares.

Over time, the Light inside helps clear out the old karma that may be causing your nightmares. Work with the HU and the MAHANTA, and know that, in time, your nightmares will stop.

Begin Your ECK Dream Study

To help you move into a higher state of awareness, try combining your contemplations with your dreams.

Love lets us enter the awakened dream state.

To begin your contemplation, shut your eyes, and place your attention on your Spiritual Eye. It is at a point just above and behind your eyebrows, and it lets us see with our inner vision. Look gently at an imaginary screen, and softly sing *God*, *HU*, *Mahanta*, or *Wah Z*.

Watch as the Blue Light appears on your inner screen. This is the Light of God. You may also hear the Sound. It could be almost any sound of nature or musical instrument that you can imagine. When the Light and Sound appear, you are in contact with the Voice of God.

The second part of this exercise is for the dream state. Before going to sleep, sing one of the words given above for a few minutes. When you are ready for sleep, imagine you are walking in a park or watching a quiet sunset with someone you love. Hold this vision until you fall asleep. A loved one can open your heart and wash away any fear. Love lets us enter the awakened dream state.

Whatever happens in your contemplation or your dream state, write or draw a picture of it in your dream journal.

This is a good way to start exploring the dream teachings of ECK.

Dreaming to Explore the Spiritual Laws

Did you know that there are spiritual laws of life—wonderful truths that can help you understand and meet the challenges of life and become the captain of your own destiny?

Become the captain of your own destiny.

Knowing these laws allows us to make the best choices every moment. How can you make these laws a part of your life and live in harmony with them?

Try this exercise!

Listen inwardly for the MAHANTA's guidance, and choose one of the spiritual laws from the book *The Spiritual Laws of Life* to learn about in your dreams.

For several days, read a passage on that law each night before bed. Then sing *HU*, close your eyes for sleep, and imagine yourself going to a Temple of Golden Wisdom to have an experience connected with that spiritual law.

In the morning, record anything you remember or anything that occurs to you upon waking. Also, watch your daily life as the MAHANTA helps you learn about Soul's relationship with this spiritual law.

Insights will come.

How to Have a Waking Dream

The waking dream is one of the ways the ECK can speak to you in your waking life. It is a spiritual insight that the MAHANTA gives you, usually through an outer example—something you experience in your daily life.

The spiritual life is much broader than just the dream state. Since you do not always remember your experiences on the inner planes, you may feel you are not making any spiritual progress—but that's not true.

See the connection between your inner and outer lives.

A waking dream helps you see the connection between your inner and outer lives. It can help you better understand a dream, confirm a spiritual lesson you are learning, help you find an answer to something that is troubling you, and open your awareness in any number of ways!

Try this exercise if you would like to experience a waking dream. In the morning, after you wake up, pick something you need guidance on—understanding a dream or spiritual principle, dealing with a problem, or whatever. Sing *HU* for as long as is comfortable and go into contemplation. Then ask the MAHANTA to give you the guidance you need through a waking dream, or a sign, sometime during your day.

Now go about your day, and pay special attention to the experiences that come your way. The Master may even give you a special nudge. This is part of the adventure of exploring your spiritual worlds!

Keeping a Dream Journal

Find a notebook or journal you love, or decorate one to make it special to you. Use this journal just for writing or drawing your dreams every morning as soon as you wake up.

One way to open yourself to the wisdom of your dreams is to sing *HU*, either softly or silently, for a few minutes before bedtime. Then go to sleep as usual.

Open yourself to the wisdom of your dreams.

Whenever you have a dream, jot it down in your dream journal. Describe the dream, and write down your feelings about what it may mean. Some people voice-record their dreams. Others wake up at night and fix one or two points of their dream in their mind, then write the dream down later.

Write simply. A dream may have so many details in it that you can become sidetracked from the point. To avoid this, write the dream out in full. Then put it away. At the end of the month, make believe you are an editor of a magazine. Review the inner experiences that stand out, and simplify them.

If you put any time at all into doing this dream exercise, you will begin to see how Divine Spirit is using your dreams to bring you spiritual understanding. The spiritual program of ECK dream study can help you find peace of mind.

The Radio-Host Technique

If you have a bad dream that you don't understand or that leaves you unsettled when you wake up, try this four-step spiritual exercise to get the rest of the story.

First, go into contemplation, and imagine turning on a radio. Listen for the sound of the radio host's voice.

Second, listen to the host telling you the details of your dream up to the time you woke up. This is a basic summary of your dream.

Listen for the rest of the story.

Third, take a "commercial break," and while it's going on, sing *HU*. At some point, the host returns and says, "And now, here's the rest of your dream."

Finally, imagine the radio host telling you the rest of the story, taking you to the next step in getting a spiritual understanding of your dream.

Reversing a Bad Dream

When you have a bad dream and wake up afraid or angry, you can imagine yourself changing the dream's ending.

For instance, if you dream you are in a dark building, imagine walking out of the building into the sunlight. Imagine yourself moving from a lower, darker world into a higher, lighter one. When you do this, you may suddenly understand the meaning of the dream.

You have the power to change your dreams.

Record the dream's meaning and new ending in your dream journal.

Remember, when you have a dream that you would like to change, you can go into contemplation and use this technique to take the dream one step further. As Soul you have the creative power to change your dreams!

What's Your Question?

At some level Soul knows everything. But is there a question on your mind—something you would like to bring into your awareness? Here is a way to get help.

Before you go to sleep, relax and decide that when you wake up, you will have an answer to whatever question you may have.

At some level Soul knows everything.

When you wake up, your answer will be in the forefront of your thoughts. There is a moment, as you slip from or into sleep, when you are opened to truth and are in direct contact with it. That is the moment when you can receive your answer.

Write it down! Make note of any answer, thought, feeling, or idea in your dream journal. Doing this is a way of saying, "Thank you" and keeping the channel open.

When You Are Too Busy

When your schedule doesn't allow time for you to sit and do a twenty-minute spiritual exercise, you can try a technique that I have used fairly often myself.

Just before you go to sleep, you can say to the Inner Master, "I give you full permission to take me to the place that I have earned or where I can learn something." Then go to sleep, and don't give it another thought.

The Inner Master can work with you in your dreams.

The Inner Master will begin working with you in your dreams. Often you will find that as your consciousness changes, your outer life may change too. It may take a couple of years. This is the physical world, and things often take some time.

But the ECK Masters begin working with us where they find us. In the spiritual works, we begin at the point where we are. Today. Right now.

The ECK will take you one step at a time inwardly, and this will reflect outwardly in your daily life in some way. Your life may not be easier, but it will certainly become more adventuresome.

Journal Your Experience

Write or draw anything you see, feel, hear, or experience during your spiritual exercise.

Journal Your Experience

Write or draw anything you see, feel, hear, or experience during your spiritual exercise.

ECK MASTERS

AND YOU

Contemplation Seeds

Many of you have been students
of one or more of the ECK Masters
in a past lifetime.

The ECK Masters walk among you now,
today, ready to serve as your friends,
teachers, guides, and protectors.

Whether male or female,
all ECK Masters awaken a
deep longing for Sugmad (God) in you.

The ECK Spiritual Guides
come by day, by night, at times of
great trouble or need, or in disguise to
bring comfort to an old friend—
perhaps someone like you.

Learn from an ECK Master

Many people around the world meet the ECK Masters long before they ever hear about Eckankar.

There is no limit to the kind of help the ECK Masters can give. They awaken people to the fact that there is more to life than meets the eye. Sometimes people see them as guardian angels. Or an ECK Master might appear to a child as an invisible friend. Other times, they will appear physically to give help during a time of intense need, then disappear.

There is no limit to the help ECK Masters can give.

Above all, the ECK Masters have dedicated themselves to helping Soul realize Its divine nature and fulfill Its highest destiny—to become a Coworker with God.

* * *

Today, choose one of the ECK Masters to act as your inner companion for the day.

Take a little time to read a description of that ECK Master or a story about the Master's life in *Those Wonderful ECK Masters, ECK Masters and You: An Illustrated Guide*, or another ECK book. Then sit down, and sing the ECK Master's name as a mantra. A mantra is a spiritual word to chant that heightens your awareness of the ECK, the God Current.

Imagine the ECK Master you've chosen paying you a visit. Greet the Master, and begin a friendly conversation. Is there something you would like to know? Go ahead and ask! Then listen inwardly for the answer the Master gives. What does the ECK Master tell you? Does the Master take you somewhere or teach you something new?

Remember this ECK Master's presence with you throughout the day. Be open to how this Master is showing you something in your life that can help you take another spiritual step on *your* journey home to God.

Meet Fubbi Quantz

Try this spiritual exercise to meet ECK Master Fubbi Quantz. He served as the MAHANTA, the Living ECK Master during the time of Buddha, around 500 BC, and is now the guardian of the Shariyat-Ki-Sugmad at the Katsupari Monastery. This monastery is located on the physical plane in northern Tibet, hidden from human eyes to keep it protected.

Good humor gleams in his eyes.

* * *

To meet Fubbi Quantz, sing *HU* softly with your eyes closed. Imagine a large, round room with a vaulted ceiling high above you. The Light and Sound of God moves through the room in gentle rhythms, bathing you with Its healing and restorative powers. Look around as you enter this room. What color is it? What furniture do you see? Is there a certain scent?

Fubbi Quantz waits for you in the room. He is a tall, elderly man with white hair and beard and a gentle smile. He wears a long white robe that falls well below his knees, and good humor gleams in his eyes.

He invites you to lie down on a special healing bed that looks as though it would be hard and uncomfortable, yet you find it surprisingly comfortable. Feel the soothing currents of the ECK wash over you as you lay there resting. This experience may leave you feeling renewed and stronger in body and spirit.

You may also ask Fubbi Quantz a question if you wish. The answer will often come later, after you've finished your contemplation and have returned to the waking state. It may come when you are reading from your ECK discourse or one of the ECK books. You might also hear Fubbi Quantz's gentle voice whisper the answer in your ear.

Listen and be aware until the answer comes. For it surely will.

Meet Gopal Das

Would you like to meet the great ECK Master Gopal Das? He was the MAHANTA, the Living ECK Master in Egypt around 3000 BC, when the pharaohs were building pyramids at Saqqara. In fact, it was Gopal who inspired the Egyptian book of dreams, one of the oldest books known to humankind. He now teaches at the Temple of Askleposis on the Astral Plane. You may recognize him by his long golden hair, and he often wears a white or maroon robe.

Patience and determination go a long way toward success.

* * *

If you would like to meet him, here is a way you can.

First, sit in a comfortable chair with your eyes closed. Then imagine yourself in a land with a warm, dry climate, where the air is sweet and fresh and the sky is a brilliant blue. Everything else in sight is a pleasant golden color.

Sing the word *Gopal* (GOH-pahl) for five to ten minutes. Then, quick as a wink, see yourself in a high spiritual world with Gopal Das. Look around yourself. What do you see? Pay close attention to the ECK Master. What is he wearing? Look into his bright blue eyes as he softly smiles at you. Then go with him as he takes you to a Temple of Golden Wisdom or on some other adventure. Where do you go?

It may take a bit of time to catch on to how simple this spiritual exercise is, but stay with it. Patience and determination go a long way toward success.

Have fun traveling with Gopal on the inner planes!

Meet Kata Daki

The ECK Master Kata Daki is one of the better-known female ECK Masters. Though her true age is beyond human understanding, she appears to be around thirty years old. She is of average height and has light-brown or honey-blond hair. With her profound kindness, wisdom, and compassion, Kata Daki serves all states of consciousness, from the highest to the lowest, and inspires in others a deep longing for God. If you'd like, she can help you learn the secret of love.

She can help you learn the secret of love.

* * *

First, take these words to heart. They're from *The Shariyat-Ki-Sugmad*, Book One: "Love does not come to those who seek it, but to those who give love." Now shut your eyes in quiet contemplation. Then sing the word *seva* (see-VAH), a spiritual word that means a service of love.

Imagine Kata Daki walking toward you. You have an appointment with each other. As she approaches, ask her to show you how to give love to others in ways you may not have thought of before. She smiles at you and shares a great secret about love. She may remind you of a time you received divine love when you were in need. Then she asks you how you would like to return that gift of love to others. Take a moment to contemplate her question before you answer. You'll think of ways you've never before imagined!

Enjoy speaking with her about any other question in your heart. You'll be glad you did.

Meet Lai Tsi

Lai Tsi is the ECK Master who serves as the guardian of the Shariyat-Ki-Sugmad in a Temple of Golden Wisdom on the Etheric Plane. Long ago, he served as the MAHANTA, the Living ECK Master in ancient China. He is a slender man of medium height, has a white beard, and usually wears his hair in a single braid. He often wears a maroon robe and a high, brimless hat that has mysterious symbols on it. He has dark, shining eyes and a wide, happy smile that is full of joy.

Learn about living the high path of ECK.

* * *

If you would like to meet Lai Tsi, look at the drawing of him at the top of this page. Study it for a few moments. Then close your eyes and gently sing his name, Lai Tsi (lie TSEE), very slowly as you picture the ECK Master's face before you on the screen of your inner vision.

There may be a humming sound like the

buzzing of bees or a soft, silvery light. Pay attention to anything and everything you see and hear.

Lai Tsi may suddenly appear before you and greet you. What does it sound like when he says your name? Notice his graceful hands and his beautiful, embroidered jacket. Carefully study every detail about him, especially the light of ECK in his eyes.

Lai Tsi may take you to read from the Shariyat, which rests on a lectern far below a radiant ball of golden light. Or perhaps he will introduce you to some animal friends he has brought with him. Let your experience unfold as it will.

What does he teach you about living the high path of ECK? In your daily life, practice kindness toward people, animals, and even plants. Inwardly ask Lai Tsi to show you ways you may have overlooked. He will be happy you asked!

Meet Paul Twitchell

Would you like to meet Paul Twitchell, the ECK Master who reintroduced the teachings of Eckankar in modern times? Paul is of medium height, with a round face and piercing blue eyes. He studied with the great ECK Master Rebazar Tarzs, who helped prepare him to become the MAHANTA, the Living ECK Master in 1965. His spiritual name is Peddar Zaskq.

Here is a spiritual exercise to try if you would like to meet him.

Let him guide you to jewels of wisdom.

* * *

As you lie in bed ready for sleep at night, picture a library on the inner screen of your mind. Imagine a large, beautiful, quiet library with tall shelves. Notice how the rows of books glow with soft light.

Now sing *HU*. Fill yourself with love as you sing this ancient name for God.

As you sing, tiptoe among the books until you find Peddar Zaskq working away at a desk, bathed in a golden light. His sparkling blue eyes will greet you as he looks up. Ask him any spiritual question you would like the answer to, and let him guide you to the jewels of wisdom around you. Where do you find your answer?

Meet Rami Nuri

Rami Nuri is the ECK Master who serves as guardian of the Shariyat-Ki-Sugmad, the sacred scriptures of ECK, at the House of Moksha, a Temple of Golden Wisdom located in the city of Retz on Venus. This spiritual site is a supraphysical one, which means it exists above the normal range of human perception. It is cloaked to human eyes because of its high vibrations.

Rami Nuri is a tall, well-built, noble-looking man with white hair and a neatly trimmed white beard. The letter *M* appears on his forehead.

Your experience will be one of a kind!

* * *

To make the inner journey to meet Rami Nuri, get comfortable, close your eyes, and put your full attention on the Spiritual Eye, found between and behind the eyebrows. Then begin to softly sing *Moksha-alayi*

(MOHK-shah ah-LAH-yee). Sing this word for five to ten minutes with a sweet love for God in your heart. This love will act as a magnet that draws you to your goal of meeting Rami Nuri.

Now imagine a dome-shaped structure made of a see-through material that echoes with the ECK Sound Current. This is the House of Moksha, which means "house of liberation."

The MAHANTA, the Living ECK Master is standing there beside you. He tells you how to bring your vibrations into harmony with this Golden Wisdom Temple and prepare to receive the wisdom found there.

When you are ready, Rami Nuri will approach, and the MAHANTA will introduce you to him.

It may take more than one attempt to meet Rami Nuri. But keep at it. You can succeed if you really want to. Your experience will be one of a kind!

When you succeed, remember to record whatever happens in your journal.

Meet Rebazar Tarzs

Rebazar Tarzs served as the MAHANTA, the Living ECK Master during the Middle Ages. He is said to be over five hundred years old and has been the spiritual teacher of many ECK Masters. Today, he lives in a hut in the Hindu Kush Mountains. He serves as the Torchbearer of Eckankar, the one who steps in as the MAHANTA if ever the current Living ECK Master departs before his successor receives the Rod of ECK Power on October 22.

He serves as the Torchbearer of Eckankar.

Nearly six feet in height, Rebazar has a full, thick, neatly trimmed black beard and dark eyes that are full of love and compassion. He is strong and deeply tanned, and he often wears a maroon robe, though he can appear in any type of clothing. Like all ECK Masters, he assists the current Living ECK Master and has dedicated his entire life to helping Souls find their way home to God.

If you would like to meet this magnificent ECK Master, get comfortable, and close your eyes. Relax in contemplation, and picture yourself walking along a beach. As you walk in the sand at the ocean's edge, the warm waters lap around your feet, and a light ocean spray splashes a refreshing coolness on your face. Overhead, white seagulls sail upon the wind.

Breathe in as the waves gently wash toward you. Then, on the outgoing breath, sing *Rebazar* (REE-bah-zahr) softly in rhythm with the waves that are making their way back to the sea.

What is his gift to you?

Continue walking until you see a figure sitting at a campfire up ahead. As you approach, you see that it is Rebazar Tarzs. He invites you to join him at the fire. He hands you a special object he's found at the beach. It may be something from the ocean that carries a special meaning for you. A starfish, a shell, or an oyster with a pearl. Or even a star he has plucked from the night sky.

What is Rebazar's gift to you?

When you return from your contemplation, write down anything you remember.

At first you may feel you have met Rebazar only in your imagination. But with time and practice, you will find that he and the other ECK Masters are real people just like you.

Meet Shamus-i-Tabriz

Would you like to meet ECK Master Shamus-i-Tabriz? He was the Outer and Inner Master of ECK in thirteenth-century Persia, and he was also the spiritual teacher of the Persian poet Jalal ad-Din ar-Rumi. Today, he serves as guardian of the Shariyat-Ki-Sugmad in the Temple of Sakapori on the Causal Plane.

His voice makes the love of God dance in your heart.

And how would you recognize Shamus? He is a broad, heavyset man of medium height and appears to be about forty. He has dark hair, a full, short, brown beard, and dark, flashing eyes. He generally wears a maroon robe and a white turban, though he sometimes sports a floppy, wide-brimmed hat. The scent of jasmine often accompanies him.

* * *

To meet this remarkable ECK Master, close your eyes and begin to softly sing *HU*.

Imagine you're in a vast, golden desert. It

is early morning, and you can see the sun rising over the sand dunes in the distance.

Listen for the sound of tinkling bells as you look for a moving figure on the horizon. As the figure draws closer, you may hear the deep laughter of the ECK Master Shamus-i-Tabriz rippling out to greet you.

Open your heart to this familiar, ancient friend.

Open your heart to this familiar, ancient friend. You're in good company. Walk with him across the desert sand, and speak comfortably with him about your spiritual goals.

Now listen with the ears of Soul. Everything he says makes the love of God dance in your heart.

Be sure to write down whatever Shamus shares with you. It will change you in a positive way.

Meet Towart Managi

Would you like to meet Towart Managi?

There are many ECK Masters of every race. The most well-known black ECK Master spoken of in the ECK writings is Towart Managi. He was the MAHANTA, the Living ECK Master in Abyssinia, an ancient African kingdom in what is now Ethiopia. Today, he is the ECK Master in charge of the Shariyat-Ki-Sugmad on the Mental Plane. His title is the Koji Chanda. He has closely cropped hair and a short white beard.

He can lead you to the Shariyat on the Mental Plane.

* * *

To meet this ancient ECK Master, sit in a quiet place, close your eyes, and gently focus your full attention on your Third Eye. It is located in the center of your head, behind and between your eyebrows. It is also called the Spiritual Eye and serves as a window between our physical world and the inner worlds of God.

Now, softly chant the word *aum*. It is the key to gain access to the Mental Plane. After a while, you may hear the sound of running water, and the ECK Master Towart Managi will appear. Ask him to take you to the Shariyat-Ki-Sugmad on the Mental Plane.

The Shariyat may appear to you as a book, a field of glowing white light, or even as heavenly music or magnificent images of some kind. However it shows itself to you, you'll be able to understand the divine messages it offers. Just open your heart to God's love.

Meet Yaubl Sacabi

Yaubl Sacabi heads the Temple of Golden Wisdom in the spiritual city of Agam Des, in the Hindu Kush Mountains of central Asia, and he is guardian of the section of the Shariyat-Ki-Sugmad located there. Long ago, he served as the MAHANTA, the Living ECK Master among the ancient Greeks; his influence at that time gave rise to a far more advanced Greek civilization. Easy to recognize, Yaubl is a strong and sturdy individual of average height, with a bald head and a broad, kind face.

He takes pleasure in teaching the secret laws of life.

To meet him, you are welcome to try the following spiritual exercise. He takes great pleasure in teaching you and others the secret laws of life, which wake us up to the spiritual adventure of our lives!

* * *

Before you go to sleep, close your eyes and sing *HU*, the love song to God, several times.

Then imagine you're walking along a mountain path. The sky above is a sparkling blue, and the sun warms the air all around you.

Up ahead, the path branches off in two directions. Yaubl Sacabi waits on one side. Go with him. Ask him any question you might have about the city of Agam Des or the Temple of Gare-Hira, where the Shariyat-Ki-Sugmad rests upon a sort of reading table, or altar.

Let him lead you there, and see what you find.

Be patient, and try again if this spiritual exercise shows no results the first time or two. Take your time. All important things take time and effort to achieve.

Journal Your Experience

Write or draw anything you see, feel, hear, or experience during your spiritual exercise.

Journal Your Experience

Write or draw anything you see, feel, hear, or experience during your spiritual exercise.

EXPLORE

THE GOD WORLDS OF ECK

Contemplation Seeds

In the inner worlds Soul is in
Its own element, like a fish
swimming happily in the sea.

As you explore experiences in the
other worlds, you are expanding your
spiritual awareness. Your attitudes change.
You become more diplomatic,
more mature, and more responsible.

Once you develop the sensitivity to go
into the inner worlds in the Soul body,
you will be able to see what is
coming before it happens.

The higher you go, the more you can see;
and the more you can see, the better
you are able to arrange your life.

Sounds of the God Worlds of ECK

Did you know there is a sound you can hear on each of the inner worlds? These sounds are listed on the God Worlds of ECK chart at the end of this exercise. Knowing these sounds can help you tell which plane you might be visiting in a dream or during contemplation or Soul Travel.

If you'd like to hear the sound of one of the inner planes, chant the spiritual word (see below) for the plane you would like to visit. Do this for at least ten minutes, slowly and softly. Next, sit in contemplation for another five to ten minutes, and listen for the Sounds of ECK.

Listen for the inner sounds.

Words to chant:

Alayi (ah-LAH-yee) for the Physical Plane.
Listen for the sound of thunder.

Kala (kah-LAH) for the Astral Plane.
Listen for the roar of the sea.

Mana (MAH-nah, mah-NAY, or mah-NAH) for the Causal Plane. Listen for tinkling bells.

Aum (AHM or ah-UHM) for the Mental Plane. Listen for running water.

Baju (BAH-joo) for the Etheric Plane. Listen for buzzing bees.

SUGMAD (SOOG-mahd) for the Atma Lok (Soul Plane). Listen for the single note of a flute.

Shanti (SHAHN-tee) for the Alakh Lok (*lok* means plane). Listen for the sound of the wind.

Hum (HYOOM) for the Alaya Lok. Listen for a humming sound.

Aluk (ah-LOOK) for the Hukikat Lok. Listen for a thousand violins.

Huk (HOOK) for the Agam Lok. Listen for the music of woodwinds.

HU (HYOO) for the Anami Lok. Listen for the HU.

Once you have identified that special sound, drift along with it. Imagine riding the waves of the Sound Current, and enjoy the peaceful feeling this brings. Look at the God Worlds chart on the next page. Imagine your consciousness expanding through each of the worlds of God. What do you experience? Remember to record this in your journal!

Each time you try this Soul Travel method, you will find new ways to make it special. Make a note of which ones you enjoy most and why.

There are countless ways to do a Soul Travel exercise, and Souls are always creating more. In time, you will develop your own spiritual exercises that work best for you!

The God Worlds of ECK

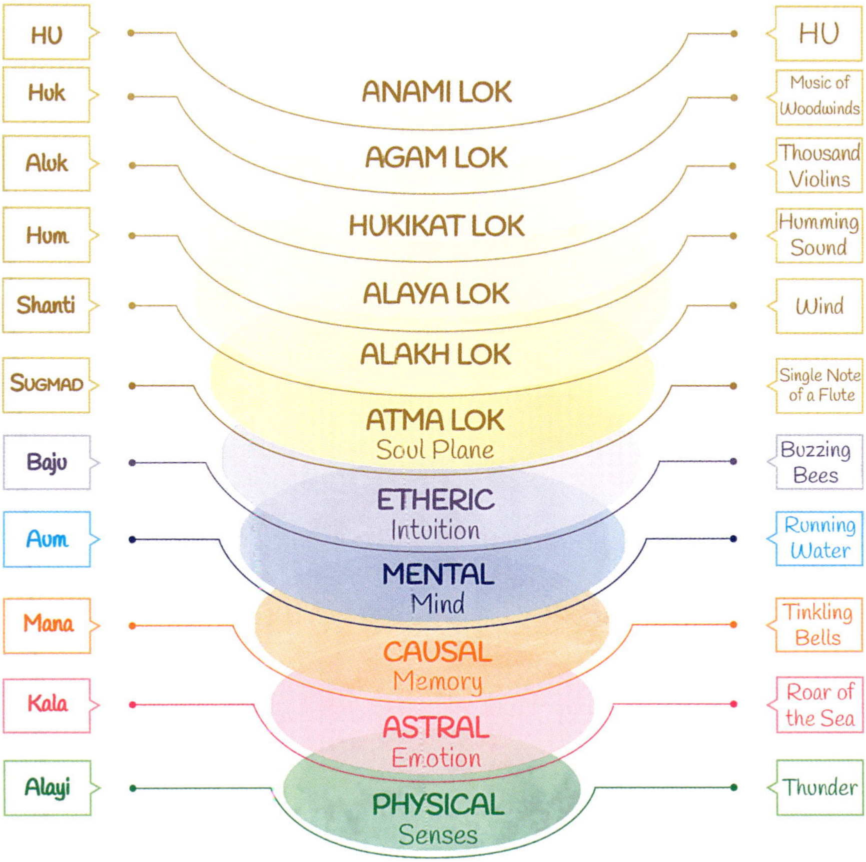

THE PURE WORLDS OF SPIRIT	Planes of God-Realization.
ATMA LOK	The Soul Plane, the plane of Self-Realization.
ETHERIC	The last barrier between the lower worlds and the pure spiritual worlds.
MENTAL	Source of all mental teachings, aesthetics, philosophies, conventional concepts of God, cosmic consciousness.
CAUSAL	Plane where memories, karmic patterns, and past-life records are stored.
ASTRAL	Plane of emotion, feelings, sentimentality. Source of all psychic phenomena—ghosts, flying saucers, spirits, ESP.
PHYSICAL	Plane where Soul learns by overcoming the five passions: lust, anger, greed, vanity, and attachment. Plane of time, space, matter, and energy.

A Golden Elevator

Begin by singing *HU* for several moments. Using your Spiritual Eye, imagine you are in the Temple of ECK and you see an ECK Master holding open the door of a golden elevator. He invites you to enter. He wants to show you something new in the God Worlds of ECK.

Take a Soul journey.

As the doors close and you begin to rise, notice how the inside of the elevator changes. It becomes larger, more spacious, and with each passing floor you can feel the speed as you whoosh upward. Your body becomes finer and sparkles with Light and Sound. When you reach your destination, the door opens.

Even though you have never consciously been there before, the room or landscape may feel familiar to you. Soul wants to explore! So step out and continue your adventure.

Tip: You might get the chance to hold a door open for someone in your day. It is a reminder from the MAHANTA of your inner journey on the golden elevator.

Journey to the Katsupari Monastery

The MAHANTA invites you to visit the Katsupari Monastery, a Golden Wisdom Temple which is located high up in the remote Buika Magna Mountains in northern Tibet.

Shut your eyes, and begin by singing *Buika Magna*. A striking mountain range may appear in your inner vision.

Imagine you are walking in these mountains with Wah Z. Your feet seem to know just where to go. As you walk the trail, you find a long set of steps cut into the rock. Look for an entrance to the Golden Wisdom Temple as you climb the steps.

Fubbi Quantz welcomes you.

You may feel a sudden rush of wind as you approach a hidden entrance. Now sing *HU*.

Inside the temple, you are welcomed by ECK Master Fubbi Quantz, who is the guardian of the Katsupari Monastery. He invites you to go explore the Temple. Where do you go first?

In one of the rooms, you will discover something of special spiritual importance for you. It might be a book, a revealing mirror, or a special garden. Or it may be something else, meant just for you.

What is it, and what does it mean for you? Whatever it is, write it down. Make it a drawing if you like. More insights will come to you as you make this record of your journey.

Visit the Astral Plane

Close your eyes, and gently chant the word *Kala* (kah-LAH) out loud for several minutes. This is the word for the Astral Plane.

Explore the Temple of Askleposis.

Look inwardly for the ECK Master Gopal Das walking toward you. He is the guardian of the fourth book of the Shariyat-Ki-Sugmad, on the Astral Plane. He invites you to the Temple of Askleposis, in the capital city, Sahasra-dal-Kanwal. The temple has a dome roof, and there are stairs leading up to the front and side doors. Gopal Das may escort you to a library, a reception hall, or a quiet alcove in a busy lobby. His company is light, kind, and uplifting.

At some point he will turn his gaze upon you. What do you see, feel, and experience? What happens next?

The Astral Museum of Inventions

To Soul Travel to another plane, all you have to do is place your spiritual attention on it.

For example, let's say that you want to go to the museum on the Astral Plane to look at inventions of the future. Inwardly invite the MAHANTA to join you on your journey. Softly sing *Kala* (kah-LAH), the spiritual word for the Astral Plane. Put your full attention on being at the museum. Here you can find inventions that have yet to be created on Earth. It is a huge building with many floors and many wondrous exhibits.

Softly sing Kala.

Take your time walking around the museum with the MAHANTA. Ask him to show you something that is significant for you today. When you come back, write or draw anything you experienced or saw in your travels.

Visit the Causal Plane

This spiritual exercise is to take you to the Causal Plane with the MAHANTA. You'll use the technique of visualization, which starts with putting your attention gently on your Spiritual Eye. This is your window to the spiritual worlds.

It is helpful to look at a picture of the MAHANTA, the Living ECK Master just before doing this spiritual exercise. It will make it easier to see him on your inner screen.

Listen for the sound of tinkling bells.

Get comfortable, and take a few gentle breaths; allow your body to relax. Then begin singing the spiritual word for the Causal Plane, *Mana* (MAH-nah, mah-NAY, or mah-NAH). The two syllables are sung slowly, out loud or silently. Sing it a few more times. Relax, and enjoy singing *Mana*.

Put the picture of the MAHANTA on your inner screen. See all his features clearly, especially his eyes. As he comes into your vision, say, "Hi, MAHANTA!" Look at his smile! Ask him if you can visit the Causal Plane. Sing *Mana* several more times, and see an orange light surround you. Step into this light. Then listen carefully for the sound of tinkling bells.

The MAHANTA will guide you on your visit to the Causal Plane, where memories and past-life records are stored. Where does he take you, and what do you see next?

Visit the Mental Plane

A way to train the mind is to use the "as if" principle. We can use the "as if" principle to change our lives and break old habits. Just imagine your goal, and act as if reaching it has already happened. Then listen to the Inner Master, the MAHANTA, for direction on the steps to take to make it an outer reality.

This is where ideas come from and thoughts are real.

You can also use the "as if" principle to Soul Travel to the Mental Plane. It's easy! The word to chant for this plane: *Aum* (AHM or ah-UHM).

While doing this spiritual exercise, look with your Spiritual Eye for the color blue. This is seeing with your inner vision. Continue to sing *Aum* several times. Then imagine being with the MAHANTA at a Golden Wisdom Temple on the Mental Plane. See the tall white columns of the Namayatan Temple up ahead.

How would you describe the Light and Sound on this plane? You may hear the sound of running water, like a mountain stream or a country creek. Or perhaps you see a white sky with a blue sun.

Enjoy your exploration of the Mental Plane. It is the home of the mind, where ideas come from and thoughts are real. Let the MAHANTA be your tour guide.

Visit the Etheric Plane

In today's spiritual exercise, visualize the Etheric Plane with all of its violet, or purple, tones. Allow your inner ears to hear the hum of the buzzing of bees.

The spiritual word for the Etheric Plane is *Baju* (BAH-joo). As you sing this word, let the two syllables come out softly. The Blue Light may appear in the Tisra Til, the Third Eye; that is the MAHANTA saying he is close by. Tell him you would like to explore the Etheric Plane. Sing *Baju* several more times, and relax in the company of the Inner Master.

Harmonize with the Sound of ECK.

The singing of *Baju*, aloud or silently within, can harmonize with the Sound of ECK and bring you to this plane of ECK love. Look for the immensely tall, beautifully rounded structure of the Dayaka Temple. Perhaps you will meet ECK Master Lai Tsi, who is the guardian of the Shariyat there.

Visit the Soul Plane

Would you like to visit the Soul Plane? In this exercise, chant the word *SUGMAD* (SOOG-mahd). It means "the all-embracing, the infinite, from which flows all life." It is another word for God, which is the Ocean of Love and Mercy, the source of all. *SUGMAD* is also the word to chant for the Soul Plane.

The spiritual vibration of the word *SUGMAD* lifts Soul into the Fifth Plane, when the MAHANTA sees that Soul is ready. The MAHANTA always guides Soul to the highest inner knowledge It can accept at any moment.

Experience yourself as Soul!

Look with your Spiritual Eye for the brilliant yellow light of this plane, and listen for the single note of a flute. The Inner Master will be at your side as you begin your explorations. You may even find yourself walking up the steps of the cylindrical Param Akshar Temple—the House of Imperishable Knowledge.

Your experience will give you a wonderful sense of your truest self, Soul.

Journal Your Experience

Write or draw anything you see, feel, hear, or experience during your spiritual exercise.

Journal Your Experience

Write or draw anything you see, feel, hear, or experience during your spiritual exercise.

Journal Your Experience

Write or draw anything you see, feel, hear, or experience during your spiritual exercise.

INNER

GUIDANCE

Contemplation Seeds

The highest truth is
not written in any book,
it's written in your heart.

You are learning how
to get your own answers
so that you can go through
life with self-mastery.

To get true inner guidance,
give God, the MAHANTA, and
yourself the purest love.
And do your
spiritual exercises in the
same spirit of love.

What's My Answer?

If you'd like to discover the answer to a problem or question via your dreams, here's an exercise to try.

Before you go to bed, get out your dream journal and a pen. Write the problem or question in your journal. Then sit in a comfortable chair, and close your eyes. Chant *HU* for a few minutes, then silently ask the MAHANTA to help you with your problem or question.

Discover your message from the ECK.

Feel the Master's love wash over you, and say, "I accept the love of the MAHANTA into my life."

When you are ready for sleep, put the open journal under your pillow, or leave it open beside your bed. Ask the MAHANTA for a dream to help answer your question or solve your problem. Also ask to remember the answer.

If you repeat this exercise for several

nights in a row and write down everything you remember each morning, you may find your answer. Or it may come during the day as a waking dream or Golden-tongued Wisdom, perhaps in something you hear on the radio or during a conversation with a friend.

It will be a message from the ECK just for you.

The Shariyat Technique

Did you know? *The Shariyat-Ki-Sugmad* means Way of the Eternal. It is the holy book of Eckankar.

This spiritual exercise can help you understand the spiritual reasons behind a problem in your life. The exercise works like this:

- Form a question about whatever is bothering you. It could be about any kind of problem.
- Open *The Shariyat-Ki-Sugmad,* Book One or Book Two, at random, and read one paragraph.
- Close your eyes, and chant *HU* as you contemplate on what you just read. It will give you one key to what you need to know about whatever is bothering you. Don't think about your problem. Just open your heart to the Light and Sound of God.

Get help to resolve a problem.

- Stay in contemplation for about five to ten minutes or so.
- Now open the *Shariyat* again at random, and read another paragraph. This paragraph will give you the second key to help resolve your problem.

This technique can be used as often as you like for more insights.

Answers before Questions

Answers to the challenges of life are always available, even before the question has been asked.

What is your question of the heart?

Close your eyes, take a few deep breaths, and relax. Imagine that you have an appointment to meet the Master on the inner planes in his study. He invites you to take a comfortable chair beside him. Before you can pose your question or speak about your problem, he hands you a beautiful sealed envelope.

What is your question of the heart?

Sing *HU,* and examine the envelope, noticing its color and the way it is sealed. Take a minute to really appreciate its beauty. There is also a special way to open this envelope. Discover what it is.

When you're ready, open it, and see what's inside. Continue to sing *HU* as you contemplate on how the contents of the envelope answer your question. What answer were you given?

The Easy Way Technique

This spiritual exercise can help you discover answers to any questions that may arise in your life.

Just before going to bed at night, place your attention on your Spiritual Eye, that place between your eyebrows. Silently, begin to chant *God* or SUGMAD.

Rely on the Inner Master.

Hold your attention on the blank screen of your inner vision, and try to keep it free of any pictures if at all possible. If you need to, when unwanted mental pictures flash up, you can replace them with the image of the Living ECK Master.

Do this exercise for ten to fifteen minutes a day. It generally won't happen overnight, but when the time is right, you will begin to see lights, usually blue or white. You will then be led to the next step to take within your own worlds. What is it? What happens when you take it?

The Easy Way technique is an opportunity to learn to rely on the Inner Master. You can mentally ask a question while you're doing this exercise, then ask it again before you drop off to sleep at night. The answer will come. Sometimes it will come in a very obvious way. Other times it may come more subtly, like through the advice of a friend, a humorous story you hear, or a symbolic dream that you develop the knack of interpreting for yourself.

List all your questions on a sheet of paper. Then continue working with this exercise. After a month, review your list to see if any of the questions have resolved themselves. Do this with all your questions every month. The results may surprise you!

If you'd like, you can send a letter to the Living ECK Master, sharing what you discover.

Golden-tongued Wisdom

The Golden-tongued Wisdom is the voice of the MAHANTA that jumps out to give you spiritual insight, help, or guidance. It usually involves voice or sound and might come through words spoken by another person in a golden moment.

Gain insight into a situation.

Its purpose is to give you insight into a situation in your life. For example, if you are wondering what to do about something, a certain word, phrase, or sentence might pop out at you from the radio or TV, as if someone just turned up the volume. The words you hear can give ideas on just what to do.

The words enter your mind and heart in a special way. You might be walking down a busy street, minding your own business, when all of a sudden you hear a person say a few words that seem unusually loud. The rest of what the person says might sound mumbled, but what they said at that moment was clear enough to stand out and mean something to you.

If you would like to experience the Golden-tongued Wisdom, start your day by singing *HU*. During your contemplation, speak to the Master about something on your mind or in your heart. Then say, "MAHANTA, if it is best for the whole, I would like to experience the Golden-tongued Wisdom today."

Keep your heart open throughout your day, listening for the moment where the MAHANTA's message reaches you through the voice of another.

Your heart will recognize a gift of inner knowing.

Making the Highest Decision

This spiritual exercise can help you stop karma before it happens.

Whenever you have to make a decision between two ways of thinking or two actions, you can stop and do a short contemplation.

Sing *HU* quietly or inwardly to yourself. Ask the MAHANTA what you could do that would put the most divine love into the situation. Sing *HU* again, and ask to be shown the effects of what you plan to do.

Stop karma before it happens.

Consider whatever you are shown or told. Then sing *HU* one last time and release it into the ECK Stream with all your love. Finish by saying, "May the blessings be."

What did you discover about the decision you need to make?

Learning to tune in to the inner guidance from the ECK and make decisions that support our highest spiritual good is an important part of our spiritual journey.

A Key from the Master

Pick one of the Master's talks to listen to. If you don't have one, you can look on Eckankar's YouTube channel.

As you listen to the Master's voice, close your eyes and imagine you are sitting in his presence, in a Temple of Golden Wisdom. Let your inner ears open to the Sound Current that flows through his voice.

Let your inner ears open.

In the Master's words you will discover a special key to help you in your life right now. You will know it when you hear it. Write it down!

The Pool of Truth

Sing *HU* softly, and become aware of the presence of the MAHANTA by your side. Ask him to show you the Pool of ECK.

In less than a second, you are in some other world. You see a small, glistening lake. It is the Pool of ECK, which is also the Pool of Truth.

Do you have a question? Ask it. Then look into the pool, and you will see truth.

See your true reflection.

As you gaze into the mirrored surface of the water, see your own spiritual reflection, clear, clean, and pure.

Take a step forward and walk into the Pool of Truth.

Feel the water gently lapping around you, and know that it is God's love surrounding you.

By doing the Spiritual Exercises of ECK, you open yourself, day by day, to receive more truth.

In time you will become the living truth yourself.

Journal Your Experience

Write or draw anything you see, feel, hear, or experience during your spiritual exercise.

Journal Your Experience

Write or draw anything you see, feel, hear, or experience during your spiritual exercise.

LIGHT-AND-SOUND-OF-GOD

ADVENTURES

Contemplation Seeds

When the Light and Sound
come into the inner vision,
the Spiritual Eye, or the heart,
you'll be filled with a joy and
love you've never felt before.

The Light of God and the
Sound of God are food for Soul.

The MAHANTA and the Light and
Sound are the same. The ECK is
the MAHANTA, the MAHANTA is the
Light and Sound, and the
Light and Sound are the ECK.
There is no separating them.

A Diamond's Reflection

Would you like to become more aware of the Light of God?

Close your eyes, and imagine you are standing with the MAHANTA, looking at a brilliant diamond. Turn the diamond around in your hand, and look at it from different angles. Tell the MAHANTA what you see. Then pass the diamond to the MAHANTA to hold.

Watch as a shaft of pure white light beams into the diamond. Thousands of twinkling lights reflect around you. As Soul, you can simply glide into the light.

The Light of God brings blessings, strength, and love.

Do you feel the joy this brings?

Listen! Do you hear the music of the Sound Current surrounding you? Allow the Light and Sound to gently wash through your whole being. It brings blessings, strength, and love. You will notice the difference.

The Voice of God

You can make contact with the Voice of God, which can be seen, heard, and felt as Light and Sound.

Close your eyes and relax. You are preparing to enter the inner temple, that sacred place where Soul has communication with God. You may see the Light of God first in your Spiritual Eye. It might appear as the Blue Light or Blue Star. Or you may see It as a globe or dot of light.

Enter an inner temple.

Seeing this means you have contact with the highest state of consciousness anywhere. Over time, the MAHANTA can uplift you to the very same state.

After you see the Light in your Spiritual Eye or feel It in your heart, then comes the Sound. Sometimes the Sound comes first.

The Sound may be the flute of God, which comes from the Soul Plane. Or you may hear the buzzing of bees or any number of different sounds. Later, as you move higher, it might come as a very high peeping sound, a single peep so high that it feels as if you can barely reach it.

The Sound you hear is the Voice of God uplifting you.

Ocean-of-Light Adventure

Close your eyes, and find your Spiritual Eye. It is right above and between your eyebrows. Now very gently look for the Light, which can come in many different ways.

At first you may see a soft glow of light that you think is just your imagination. It might appear as little blue spots of light or as a ray of light. Or it could look like a beam of light coming through an open window from the sunshine outside. The white light may also show up in any number of ways.

Set no limitations.

As you look for the Light, chant your secret word or *HU*, a sacred name for God. Watch as this Light turns into an ocean of light. Then look for a little boat that's coming to shore very near where you're standing. At the helm is the MAHANTA or one of the ECK Masters, who invites you into the boat. Don't be afraid; just get in! It is an exciting moment for Soul!

When you get to this point, just follow whatever experience comes to you. Set no limitations on it. You may end up in a video arcade, or you may end up inside a Temple of Golden Wisdom. Or you may have an experience with the Light and Sound of God coming directly into Soul.

Enjoy your special journey!

Your Cup of Living Water

Chant the word *SUGMAD* out loud or to yourself. Picture a desert with a green oasis in the middle. As you walk through this oasis, you see people from many cultures and religions standing in line, with cups in their hands. You are also holding a cup. You get in line too.

Continue to chant *SUGMAD*. You see that the Living ECK Master waits at a well. As each person offers his empty cup, the Master fills it lovingly from the well of Living Water, which is the ECK Itself. Very soon it is your turn, and the Master recognizes you. He gives you a special smile and says your name. After he fills your cup, drink the Living Water to the last drop, with thanks and joy in your heart.

Awaken the God knowledge within you.

As you drink, imagine the Light and Sound of God rushing through your whole being. Know that once you drink this water, you will never be the same. It will begin to awaken the God knowledge already in your heart.

Experience in the Light and Sound of God

Close your eyes, and listen for the ECK Sound Current. It can be heard within outer sounds like the humming of a refrigerator or air conditioner. It is in the sound of the wind in the leaves, falling rain, thunder of jets, singing birds, and the awful rumble of a tornado. Again, Its sound can be heard in laughter, weeping, the din of city traffic, ocean waves, and the quiet rippling of a mountain stream. It can also be heard as an inner sound.

Energize every atom in your being!

Listen to the sounds around you, and relax into the rhythm of the current. Listen for the Sound behind all sounds.

When you are ready, look for the inner light. The Light of God can appear in any color and in many ways. You may see a twinkle or flash of light, a small dot, or a radiant beacon shining bright!

Sing *HU*, and see the Light of God on your inner screen. Let its warmth envelop you.

As the Light and Sound swirl around and within you, feel them energizing every atom in your being. Enjoy this experience of God's love!

Afterward, pay close attention to your dreams, spiritual exercises, and physical life. How does the Light and Sound show up in your day-to-day life?

Listening to the Night

When you go to bed, listen in a gentle way to the night sounds. Sometimes you'll hear the night birds, the hum of air conditioning, the traffic outside, a helicopter flying overhead, or the soft rumble of voices. Just lie in bed and listen. You hear these different sounds so often that you usually tune them out. Put some attention on them now.

Hear the sacred sounds of ECK.

While you listen to these physical sounds, sing *HU*, and then listen for the sacred sounds of ECK. They come in many forms, sometimes as the ringing or tinkling of bells or the sound of musical instruments.

Try to identify as many different physical sounds as you can. Go to sleep with these sounds in your consciousness, knowing they are part of HU, the universal God Sound which contains all other sounds.

Listen carefully, because in these sounds you will find this secret name of God. The Light and Sound are God's way of speaking directly to you, to Soul!

Journal Your Experience

Write or draw anything you see, feel, hear, or experience during your spiritual exercise.

Journal Your Experience

Write or draw anything you see, feel, hear, or experience during your spiritual exercise.

MEET THE

MAHANTA

Contemplation Seeds

The journey home to God
begins with meeting the MAHANTA
either in a dream or in person.

As Soul, you have the God knowledge within you. My main job is to awaken the knowledge and love for the divine things that are already in your heart.

The MAHANTA, the Living ECK Master is a Wayshower. He is not a way-pusher or a way-dragger who kicks and shoves you through the inner worlds. The Wayshower is simply someone who shows you the way.

Look for the ECK in the face of all you meet, for then you will see the face of the MAHANTA, the face of love. Love is what opens all doors for you, everywhere, in all the worlds.

Travel the Highway of Silvery Stars

When we sing *HU* and ask to go traveling with the MAHANTA, almost anything can happen. Read this poem by a young ECK chela, which was published in the *Letter of Light*. Then imagine the Master asking you, "Would you like to come traveling with me?"

"Would you like to come traveling
with me?" he asks.
I blink in surprise,
Open my inner eyes.
The choice is mine
To go or to stay,
To spend this moment of the day
Exactly as I choose.
"Oh, yes!" I say,
"With all my heart."
Reach out my hand to clasp the hand
of the MAHANTA
And together we walk up a highway
paved with silvery stars.

See where the Master takes you!

Sing *HU* and imagine stepping onto a highway of silvery stars. Then follow the Master, and see where he takes you!

The Darshan

What is your favorite picture of the Master, the one that most touches your heart? In a quiet, private place and time, look at this image, or just use your Spiritual Eye to picture the Master. You can also use the illustration on page ix, in the front of this book.

Experience the Gaze of the Master.

Look into his eyes, and see him looking at you—into you—with pure love and delight. Quietly sing *HU* or *Darshan*.

Feel the truth of the MAHANTA's love for you, beyond time, beyond words, beyond questions or thoughts. This is the Darshan, the Gaze of the Master.

It is a recognition of the heart and a joy of Soul. His gaze says, "I am always with you."

Building Your Relationship with the Mahanta

Would you like to have an inner experience with the Mahanta or build an even stronger relationship with him?

As a student of Eckankar, you can connect with the Mahanta, the Living ECK Master anytime just by turning your attention to him. You can also look for him through your Spiritual Eye. You may see him as a blue, white, or yellow light or star. You might hear him speak to you or just get a feeling of what he is trying to tell you. You may feel a gentle nudge or hear his voice as the inner whispering of your heart.

Imagination is a good place to start your communication with the Mahanta. Use your creativity to imagine the Inner Master walking and talking with you. Practice holding conversations with him, and one day you

Use your creativity.

will suddenly realize that what began as imagination is now a very real experience.

Do this every day so that talking and listening to the Master will become as natural as talking and listening to yourself or anyone.

Getting to know the Inner Master is just like getting to know a new person at school. Be patient, and your awareness will grow.

Invite the Dream Master

The Dream Master, who is really the MAHANTA, the Living ECK Master, works with the dreamer when invited in some way.

If you want to work with the Dream Master while you sleep, try this exercise!

Before going to sleep, inwardly give permission to the Dream Master to be with you. Imagine placing all your problems and concerns in his hands, and let your mind let go of all worries. Ask the Dream Master to help clear up any karma that is standing in the way of your spiritual growth.

Let your mind let go of its worries.

Then go to sleep, aware that you are resting in the care of the Dream Master, who will look out for you and take you on a journey for your spiritual unfoldment.

In the morning, write down any feelings you have upon waking or any dream you remember.

Practice the Presence

This spiritual exercise is to help you practice the spiritual presence of the Living ECK Master. Each week for the next month, pick a special way to remind yourself of his love and presence!

It could be as simple as drawing a blue star or *Z* on your thumbnail or setting an alarm in your phone to remind you to place your attention on the MAHANTA. Be as creative as you like!

For example, the first week you might put a picture of the Master under your pillow or by your bedside. The second week, you could pick a sound to remind you of the Living ECK Master, such as a bird chirping or a horn honking. The third week, you might sing *Wah Z* each night. Or you could try singing *Z* whenever you see the color blue. The fourth week, you could write a few sentences to the Master every day. Then, if you'd like, at the end of the week you can send what you wrote to Sri Harold Klemp at PO Box 2000, Chanhassen, MN 55317-2000.

See, hear, and feel the MAHANTA's love.

What creative techniques work for you?

The MAHANTA is always as close as your own heartbeat. With practice, you can learn to see, hear, and feel his presence and love in your life.

Satsang with the MAHANTA

What spiritual quality do you have a desire to demonstrate in your daily living? Compassion? Silence? Selflessness? You are invited to a Satsang class led by the Inner Master on your chosen quality. It is being held on the inner planes, in a spacious, circular room with a high, domed ceiling.

Gain unexpected freedom.

You'll be among friends. There's a special seat waiting for you. Sit down. Get comfortable. Then chant the word *Satsang* as you go into contemplation and join the class. Listen to what is being said, and ask or share whatever you wish. What interests you the most?

In your daily life, consciously practice the spiritual quality you focused on. It will bring unexpected freedom in some area of your life, inwardly or outwardly.

Listening for HU

Sit quietly, and close your eyes. Sing *HU* for a few moments. Imagine meeting with the MAHANTA on the inner planes, somewhere you have never visited in a spiritual exercise before—perhaps a waterfall, a bonfire at the ocean, or a mountain lookout. Where are you? What do you see?

Hear the God Sound.

Sit with the Master, and listen to any sounds you hear around you.

The Master listens with you and then reveals how each sound comes from HU, the God Sound. He will teach you how to hear this any moment of your day. Even in your own voice!

The Radiant Form of the Master

The MAHANTA is the inner form of the Living ECK Master, the radiant form. When you are able to view and speak with the MAHANTA, you can travel with him in your inner worlds. You can practice this now.

Walk with the MAHANTA.

Close your eyes, and sing *HU* or your secret word. Visualize the MAHANTA, the inner form of the Living ECK Master, gleaming like a thousand stars in the night. In contemplation, take a walk with him into the spiritual worlds. Notice the landscape, the color of the light, any winds or sounds. Take a moment to ask the MAHANTA any question you may have, or tell him something from your heart. Listen for his response. It may come as a gentle feeling or a knowingness.

Enjoy the companionship of the Master. It can be as natural as a feeling of comfort and love or joy in your heart.

To Hear the Master's Voice

On a piece of paper, write, "MAHANTA, I know you are here. I love you, and I am listening for your voice." Then put the paper in your dream journal, or tape it to your bedroom door or someplace you will see it every day. Each day, before doing your spiritual exercise, read those words aloud.

Listen for the whispers in your heart.

Watch your daily experiences for signs, and know that you are learning more about the MAHANTA's presence in your daily life. Listen for the Master's nudges, guidance, and whispers in your heart. Whatever you hear, write it down in your journal.

In time, you will begin to hear the Master's voice more and more clearly.

To Speak and Listen with Love

Take several deep, relaxing breaths. Begin by singing Z, and imagine you are meeting the Master by the shore of an ancient river. He invites you to talk about anything at all of interest or concern to you.

The Inner Master can hear you.

What would you like to say? Begin to speak from your heart, gently, out loud, knowing the Inner Master can hear you completely. Say all you wish to say.

Then listen, listen, and listen.

What does the Master say to you?

As you listen with your heart, you may get a sudden understanding of the true relationship between Soul and the Master. Contemplate whatever comes to you.

Later, as you go through your day, really listen to the people you encounter. Listening to others is a way to listen to the MAHANTA. Look for these divine opportunities to give and receive the Master's love throughout your day.

Journal Your Experience

Write or draw anything you see, feel, hear, or experience during your spiritual exercise.

Journal Your Experience

Write or draw anything you see, feel, hear, or experience during your spiritual exercise.

PAST LIVES,

PRESENT LESSONS

Contemplation Seeds

When we practice the Spiritual Exercises of ECK, the Inner Master will open us up to those things that are important to see about our past lives.

You can go back; pick up the tool, talent, or lesson from a previous lifetime; and bring it into the present. You can then use it to help you walk the spiritual path to God today.

Our past lives are part of what formed us in this lifetime and put us in the circle of people with whom we find ourselves today.

No matter what we were in the past during any other life, we are spiritually greater today.

Past-Life Clues

Our character is made up of virtues and shortcomings we developed in past lives. Traumas from a past life can influence how we act today. Positive experiences we've had also shape our behavior in this life.

What has shaped your character?

On the next page, make a list of people and things you like or dislike. Also note if you feel a special attraction to some country, locale, or time period in history. There is a reason for such interest.

When you look at the list, what do you notice? Next, pay attention to your dreams to see if you make any past-life discoveries there. The MAHANTA will guide you as you study your past lives, and you'll discover more about yourself as Soul.

Likes	Dislikes

Atlantis, Past and Present

The lost continent of Atlantis was home to a great civilization about twenty-five to thirty thousand years ago. It still often fascinates people who had lifetimes during that era.

Illuminate past-life talents and lessons.

The Atlanteans spoke a mixture of Lemurian and what was earlier considered a Scandinavian dialect. They were great sailors and traded abroad with what remained of the old empire of Lemuria, around the areas of the China Sea and the Far East.

Would you like to know more? Go into contemplation, and chant the word *ECK-Vidya*. Ask the MAHANTA to show you any past life you may have had in Atlantis and give you clues about how that life may be affecting your life today.

Imagine he escorts you to a library on the inner planes and hands you a particular book. You accept the book and notice the unique illustration on the cover. It might be a geometric symbol, a map, or the face of a person. What do you see?

There is also a word written on the cover. It may be a word for you to chant, or a key to exploring the book. Where does the Inner Master's guidance lead you?

You may discover a talent you had in that lifetime that you can use today. Exploring that Atlantean lifetime might also bring about a cleanup to some area of your present life. A relationship may improve, a karmic knot might untangle, or a solution to an old problem might become clear.

Watch your outer life for the effects of this spiritual exercise. Whatever unfolds will hold the MAHANTA's love for you.

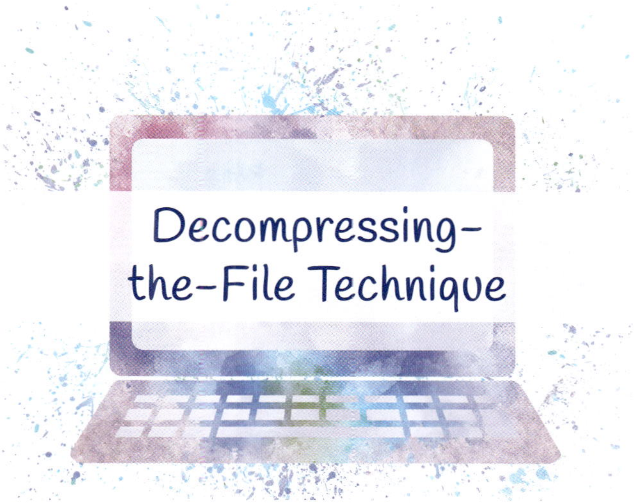

Decompressing-the-File Technique

Sometimes past-life information comes to you in the dream state. The ECK Masters can give this knowledge to you by a highly compact form of communication that is a lot like telepathy. The information is like a computer file that has been compressed for storage.

Access past-life data.

To get access to this past-life data, imagine turning on a computer or device. There is an inner message for you from the Master on it. Select it, and the computer will decompress the file so you can get the message.

The computer program will do its best to honor the contents of the Master's message as it converts the telepathic-like communication into everyday text or speech. However, no computer program is able to give an exact translation of an inner spiritual communication.

So just try to catch the spirit of the message.

Practicing this spiritual exercise is a powerful way to trigger past-life recall. It releases the invisible force that will bring you any necessary past-life recall in some way or another.

Watch your dreams for further clues, and ask the Inner Master to help you understand what is being shown and how it relates to your spiritual growth today.

Discover a Past Life

Chant the word *Mana* (MAH-nah, mah-NAY, or mah-NAH), which is the spiritually charged word to chant to visit the Causal Plane, the place of memory. Do this at least ten times.

Imagine a beautiful world with an orange sky. The MAHANTA takes your hand and guides you to the records of your past lives on Earth. You may see this as a shelf of colorful books in a library, a filing cabinet with your name on it, a movie theater showing films of your lifetimes, or whatever is right for you.

Travel to the Causal Plane.

Pay attention as the MAHANTA shows you pictures from your past lives. Look through the images. Which ones light up for you to further explore?

You can continue connecting with your past lives in the dream state at night. Before going to sleep, ask the MAHANTA to show you anything from a past life that might help you in your life today. Try this exercise at least once a week.

Be ready for experiences that will show you more about your spiritual history!

Familiar Faces and Places

Have you ever traveled to a place that felt familiar? Or met someone you felt you already knew?

When you travel to new places, waking dreams and dreams may reveal past lives you spent there. Such dreams can shed light on habits, preferences, or fears. They show things gained or lost in the past. Travel is a chance to revisit what helped make you who and what you are today. It can help remind you that you are eternal Soul and have lived before!

More clues to your past lives.

Think back to a trip you took, and ask the MAHANTA to shine a light on anything that was a clue to a past life.

What does he show you?

Ask the MAHANTA why this past life is important to you today.

What does he say?

Write down any insights you have. Then pay attention to your dreams tonight, where you may discover further clues to your past lives on earth.

When you take your next trip, make note of anything that looks or feels familiar or that you instantly love. Before you go to sleep, ask the MAHANTA to show you why it stands out to you.

Gazebo of Lifetimes

Close your eyes, and sing *Z* or *Wah Z*, Sri Harold's spiritual name, for five to ten minutes. Imagine the Inner Master walking with you toward a beautiful white gazebo set upon a sunny, grassy hill. When you climb the five steps and enter the gazebo, you see colorful mosaic art covering the walls, pillars, and domed ceiling. Each picture portrays a significant lifetime that you once lived.

Explore a significant lifetime.

Ask the Inner Master to show you which past life is especially important to you today. Explore that picture. What do you see?

Are there other people? Animals? What kind of landscape or weather? What is the story behind the picture?

Invite the Inner Master to guide your experience.

Journal Your Experience

Write or draw anything you see, feel, hear, or experience during your spiritual exercise.

Journal Your Experience

Write or draw anything you see, feel, hear, or experience during your spiritual exercise.

Journal Your Experience

Write or draw anything you see, feel, hear, or experience during your spiritual exercise.

PROBLEM

SOLVING

Contemplation Seeds

A key part of the ECK
teachings is to develop the
creative side of yourself so you
can figure out your own problems.

We learn that everything that
happens to us is to teach us more
about the laws of Spirit.

Is it true? Is it necessary?
Is it kind? Ask yourself those
three simple questions every time
you are in doubt about any action.

A solution to every problem
is within us.

Be the Cause

Contemplate on what it means to be cause rather than effect. If you are facing a difficult situation at school or in your daily life, ask yourself what actions you can take to change the way you feel about the situation.

Imagine yourself handling it with more love and confidence.

Take action.

Then release the situation to the love of the MAHANTA, and let go of the problem. Imagine the Wind of ECK blowing away any bad feelings you might have had.

This spiritual exercise brings you more spiritual freedom. Enjoy the feeling!

Conquering Fear

Embrace spiritual growth.

Sometimes when the ECK is working to bring positive changes and spiritual growth into our life, we don't quite understand what's happening or how it's going to turn out.

If you are afraid of something and feel as if you are frozen on the edge of a cliff, close your eyes and imagine the MAHANTA reaching out his hand. Visualize him guiding you past the steep ledge to where the path widens into a meadow. The path through the meadow represents the new circumstances the ECK is bringing into your life.

Then Wah Z says, "When you get to areas of the path that are unfamiliar to you, you can use a technique to help you adjust. Begin by singing *HU*. After a few minutes, you will feel less afraid. Then walk in a small circle once. Sing *HU* while you walk. This will get you used to this new area."

He shows you how to do it, and you copy him. Then he says, "Each time you walk around, make your circle a little wider. Soon you will be completely comfortable in the new area."

Try it. It works.

Stepping-Stones

Here's a spiritual exercise to look at obstacles in a whole new way. Sing *HU* quietly to yourself or out loud. Look at the obstacles in your life that you think are stumbling blocks—things that are holding you back.

Find the gift in your problems.

Now imagine the blocks becoming stepping-stones taking you higher. Where are they leading you? What are you learning about yourself?

As you sing *HU*, open yourself to a greater understanding of how these stepping-stones are helping you.

Write down what you discover about how your stepping-stones are leading you upward.

Remember to sing *HU* anytime you face a challenge or a stumbling block. You can ask the MAHANTA to show you the spiritual gift within your problem.

He'll be happy you asked!

For a New Approach to Life

Do you have a problem or a question you would like to get beyond? In contemplation, sing *HU* for several minutes, and open your heart to divine love. You can do this by thinking of someone you love or placing your attention on your love for God.

In your Spiritual Eye, see the Light of ECK entering your inner being and reorganizing the atoms of your thoughts and habits. As the sparkling Light of ECK soothes and uplifts you, allow yourself to release any attachments you have to the problem.

Reorganize the atoms of your thoughts.

Ask the MAHANTA, "What new approach can I take in my outer life to reflect this inner change?" Listen for his response.

Continue letting the Light of ECK wash through you for ten to fifteen minutes.

Watch for a feeling of lightness in your mind and heart as you go about your day.

May the Blessings Be

When you face a challenge in your life or something out in the world which you feel could use improvement, sing *H-U*, one letter at a time, aloud for several minutes. After a little while, you will feel your body relax and come into harmony with this rhythm.

In your Spiritual Eye, visualize meeting the MAHANTA by an inner fountain of Light and Sound. You may feel fountain spray upon your face or hear the water rushing like the life force through your body.

Let the ECK take charge.

Let this purifying experience bring you joy.

Later, as you go about your day, if you get distracted from the present moment by regret or sadness, practice spiritual surrender. Gently sing, "May the blessings be" as a spiritual exercise. Sing it silently or aloud for as long as you'd like, and give the situation over to the ECK with all your love and trust.

You may notice that a feeling of contentment or quiet joy enters your heart. Know that the ECK will use the situation for the spiritual benefit of everyone involved.

Snowball Technique

Have you ever tried the Snowball technique? It is a short spiritual exercise where we give a situation or problem over to the MAHANTA.

These are the steps:

1. Take a moment, with your eyes open or closed, and imagine a pile of snow.
2. Think of the problem or idea. Put it inside a snowball. Pack it tightly!
3. Now picture the ECK Stream, the river of ECK love.
4. Throw the snowball, with the problem inside, into the ECK Stream. Watch it float down the stream and disappear.
5. Then dust your hands off, and say, "That's all!" meaning that you have given it to the ECK and the MAHANTA.

Practice spiritual surrender.

Do whatever needs to be done, but do it knowing that the ECK is helping you and bringing you the experience you need at the moment.

This is a method of surrendering to the love of the MAHANTA. He is always with you. Why not accept his help? It works!

The Living ECK Master's Image

If you are ever given a responsibility, a chore, or a school project that makes you feel anxious, stressed, or pushed beyond your limits, try this spiritual exercise!

Stay centered in the Master's love.

In your inner vision, put the image of the Living ECK Master in front of you like a screen. Imagine that all thoughts, words, actions, and feelings flowing from you must pass through this screen. Likewise, all things coming toward you must pass through the image of the Master.

The image of the Master acts as a channel for the Holy Spirit to come flowing through, to lift you into the higher planes and give you greater love. Staying centered in this love can make it easier to do the things you need to do.

Tip: There's a picture of the Master in the front of this book, on page ix, that you may enjoy!

What's Perfect about This Problem?

The *Shariyat-Ki-Sugmad*, Book One, says (on page 115), "Perfection may seem far from the human state of consciousness, but one . . . can always bring out in the human self the divine Truth. He only has to be himself."

Read these words from the *Shariyat* out loud to yourself. Then take a moment to reflect on a challenging situation in your life.

Chant *HU*, and imagine you are standing with Wah Z on a mountaintop, reviewing the situation from that high spiritual perspective. He may point out certain aspects of your challenge for you to pay special attention to. Or he may replay a scene from your life (this life or a past life) that helped create the situation. Watch as he shows you how your attitude and actions can help change the way the situation turns out.

Get a spiritual perspective.

Take a moment to ask the Master any questions you may have. Then let him show you how some part of this challenge is the perfect way for you to unfold. His words will help you be your highest self.

Window of Understanding

What three positive actions can you take?

Dreams can open the window of understanding. Tonight, use your dreams to get insight into a problem or challenge.

Before bed, write your problem on a piece of paper. Write it as a question you are asking someone you trust. Then put the piece of paper under your pillow. Ask the Dream Master to show you what you need to know to see the problem more clearly.

In the morning, write or draw a picture of any feelings or experiences you had in the dream state (even if it doesn't seem to relate to the question you wrote).

Take a bit of time to contemplate this dream information. Then ask the MAHANTA for three positive actions you can take to solve the problem. Write your ideas down. How can you take those steps?

You can repeat this exercise the next day if you feel you need more insights.

The Sherlock Holmes Technique

If you have problems that you can't seem to work through, you may wish to try the following exercise.

Shut your eyes, and begin to visualize Sherlock Holmes in his funny-looking cap. First you see a luminous blue form, which then begins to look like Sherlock Holmes holding a magnifying glass in front of him, walking along a path toward you. As he gets closer, you see that he is the MAHANTA, the Living ECK Master.

Find a solution to your dilemma.

The MAHANTA greets you and then says, "If you'll come with me, we'll go find a solution to your problem."

As you begin to follow the MAHANTA, the Inner Master in the guise of Sherlock Holmes, you become more and more aware of the incredibly bright blue light around him. You also notice that the light passes through his magnifying glass like a flash-light. Together you walk through a misty marsh, and the Blue Light of ECK illuminates the path.

As you go with him, you may chant the word *HUUUACH* (HU-akh). It's similar to HU. You can use this word with this particular exercise as you are walking along with the Inner Master, who is dressed like Sherlock Holmes.

Finally you come to an enormous rock. The MAHANTA, still dressed as Sherlock, easily lifts it. He holds the magnifying glass up for you to see. The blue light shining through the glass has turned to white light. And you see the solution to your problem engraved on the bottom of the rock. What does it say?

Do this exercise every other night for one month, interchanging it with your regular spiritual exercise. It's an attempt to bypass the mind and receive insights directly from the ECK. See what you discover!

Journal Your Experience

Write or draw anything you see, feel, hear, or experience during your spiritual exercise.

Journal Your Experience

Write or draw anything you see, feel, hear, or experience during your spiritual exercise.

PROTECTION

Contemplation Seeds

You can protect yourself. Sing *HU,* the love song to God, in silence, and fix your whole inner attention upon the loving radiance of the MAHANTA. I am always with you.

Ask yourself, "Have my emotions opened the door for this power to attack me?"

After you have done everything you can do, sing *HU* quietly. Then stand back and let Spirit take charge.

When we are filled with love, the protection of the ECK comes through and helps us in our daily lives.

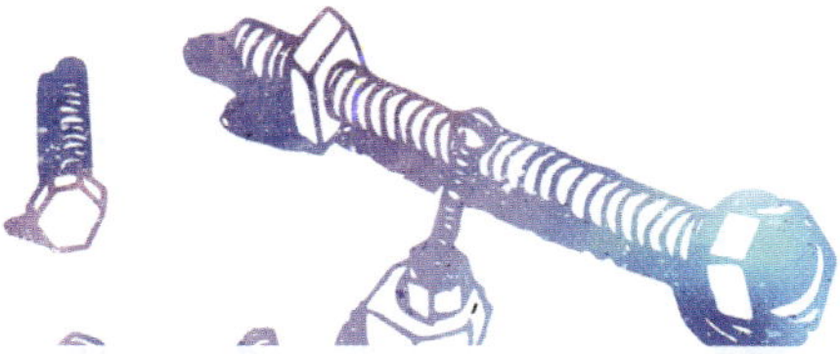

Calling upon the Little ECK Helpers

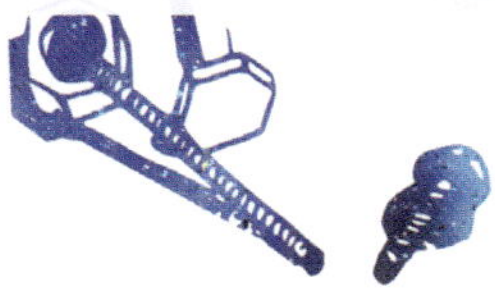

If you find yourself in a situation where you sense danger, use your imagination in contemplation to get ECK help. Open your heart to Spirit, and call upon "the little ECK helpers."

If you are on an airplane, for example, you can imagine a team of neatly uniformed little ECK workers tightening all the nuts and bolts. See them making sure all the plane's hoses and nozzles are secured. Once you let your imagination take over, all you have to do is watch them work.

Use your creative imagination.

Whenever there is a crisis, you can use this creative exercise and visualize these workers fixing whatever is wrong. It isn't limited to airplanes; it can be done anywhere, even at school or in your home.

The little ECK helpers only make things better for all concerned. They work only in a positive way.

You don't have to passively accept the difficulties that come into your life. If you receive an inner warning that something negative is about to happen, you can use your creative imagination. Know that there is a way to neutralize the experience—if it is the will of the ECK.

Depending on the situation, you may still need to take action, though. So be alert and creative on the outer too.

Cloak of Love and Protection

Many ECKists have experienced the cloak of spiritual protection. If you would like to experience it, try this spiritual exercise.

Close your eyes, and sing *HU*. Imagine the MAHANTA giving you a box tied with a ribbon made up of thousands of sparkling gold stars. The MAHANTA looks into your eyes with love as you open the box.

Inside is a beautiful cloak of sparkling gold stars like the ribbon. The MAHANTA tells you it is your cloak of love and protection. You can put it on whenever you need help. It will be invisible to others, and it will help you feel the MAHANTA's presence in any situation.

Feel the MAHANTA's presence.

When you put the cloak on, you float upward with the MAHANTA, gently and slowly. You are now able to get a better view of your situation. What does the Master show you?

You can call for help anytime, whether you are in a dream or awake. The MAHANTA will throw this protective cloak around you to keep you from spiritual harm. This special protection is divine love. The deep love between you and the MAHANTA gives you help and protection whenever you need it.

Protection against Negative Forces

HU is a powerful defense. When you find yourself in need of extra strength or protection, sing *HU* inwardly or aloud. Fill yourself with love, and bathe in the Light and Sound of God.

People all over the world sing *HU* to receive protection from trouble or danger on the street, at school, or at home.

HU also offers protection when we feel someone is inwardly attacking us. Aiming negative, harmful thoughts or intentions toward another person is a form of black magic, something an ECK chela never does. This problem is well-known in Africa, where ECKists often ask me, "How can we become strong so that no negative force can harm us?"

Nothing can hurt us unless we ourselves allow it.

The old law of protection is this: Nothing can hurt us unless we ourselves allow it. A way to protect yourself is to consciously close the emotional door against the intruder.

If you are the object of such an attack, put your full attention on the MAHANTA, and chant the word *HU*. Picture a shield of white light between yourself and the person who is causing the problem, and know that the MAHANTA is standing by your side in the form of a Blue Light.

Always remember that the ECK is stronger than any force in the lower worlds. The Light and Sound are the two most trusted pillars of protection that one can ever find.

Zipping Up Your Aura

The Shariyat-Ki-Sugmad, Book Two, says (on page 69), "An individual traveling the path of ECK soon learns that he is . . . a spiritual being with full control over his emotions and desires."

If you feel a desire or emotion you don't want or need, imagine a field of protection around yourself. It may be a powerful and impenetrable light, a barrier of sound, or a reflective shield.

Take control of your emotions.

Then look for one action you can take to protect yourself from emotional outbursts—perhaps counting to ten, repeating a favorite ECK song lyric, or imagining yourself zipping up your aura.

Look forward to this chance to exercise the freedom you have as Soul. You will feel stronger.

HU

Protection from Negative Attitudes

There are two things you can do to feel the love of God while surrounded by people with negative attitudes:

1. Be polite when these people are near you, but sing *HU*, the love song to God, silently. Listen to them while you sing *HU*, rather than getting into a long conversation with them. Say as little as possible while still remaining cordial.
2. In your imagination, see the MAHANTA near you.

The negative power is using these people as its channels to see whether you will agree with their opinions or join them in gossip. Each challenge is an opportunity to grow spiritually. Look to the MAHANTA for the strength and divine love needed to meet each spiritual test.

Look to the MAHANTA for strength.

Self-Protection

To protect yourself, remember these two principles: (1) never believe that you will be spiritually harmed by anything or anybody, because you are ageless, eternal Soul; and (2) practice fearlessness by never letting your imagination run wild and worry about something happening to harm you.

Here are three techniques you can do in contemplation for self-protection:

Practice fearlessness.

1. Place an outward-facing mirror in front of you, which anyone attacking you can see inwardly but cannot tolerate. It will reflect negative energy back to the sender.
2. Place a shield of white light around yourself.
3. Start talking in a normal voice, telling any intruding person, "You are invading my personal spiritual space. Please stop immediately."

Know the MAHANTA is with you, giving you strength, confidence, and inner guidance every step of the way.

Shield of Silver Light

In the forest of the SUGMAD, there is an enormous clearing. It is set in a breathtakingly beautiful landscape, where the sky is baby blue, speckled with fluffy white clouds.

You have the love and protection of the Holy Spirit.

Against the stump of an ancient tree, all by itself in the middle of the clearing, stands a silver shield. It appears as a mighty warrior's shield from medieval times. The Light of God shines down from above, strikes the shield, and comes off in a ray of light so brilliant that it will blind anyone who approaches it with an impure heart.

This Shield of Silver Light stands as a protection for the children of ECK, those who make the commitment to follow the high path of love. No being can approach it except in the spirit of love. And when you can approach the Shield of Silver Light in the spirit of love, you have the protection of the MAHANTA with you. Nothing can touch you, nothing can harm you.

When battle must be done to bring protection to Its own, the Inner Master, the MAHANTA, will go to the inner clearing, pick up the shield, and with the sword of the SUGMAD he will take the field in battle for you.

If you know and accept this, then you have the love and protection of the Holy Spirit against every psychic attack, against all harm and all danger. In times of danger, you have the ability to wrap this aura of love so tightly around you that nothing can touch you.

In your contemplation, see yourself walking beside the MAHANTA through the meadows to this great forest. When you reach the clearing in the middle of the forest, you will find the Shield of Silver Light, which is the shield of love. Stand within its circle of protection, and know that you are standing in the love and protection of the SUGMAD. Stay in this experience of love and protection for as long as you wish.

Washing Away Worries

There is a law in the lower worlds that if anyone responds to worry, he creates a reason for worry.

To keep yourself from worrying, sing *HU*, and bathe yourself in a waterfall of Light and Sound. Feel it cleansing away your tensions and stress. Enjoy the refreshing peace and calm.

Shift your attention to the ECK.

Now watch as the Master offers you a special kind of shield to wear as a protective buffer between you and the events of your day. It could appear as a force field of neutrality or a warm, glowing light.

What does your shield look like to you?

All you have to do to receive this protection is shift your attention to the ECK. This simple act of self-discipline activates the protection. Try it and see!

Try this exercise if you feel in need of spiritual protection. Shut your eyes at bedtime, and see yourself standing before a gigantic mountain of light. From the mountain flows the most enchanting melody of the Audible Life Stream.

Now visualize yourself walking up the sidewalk to a huge door that guards an entrance into the side of the mountain. The door's mighty construction can withstand a thermonuclear blast.

Enter, and pull the door shut behind you. Notice how easily it swings, despite its great height and massive construction. With the door shut and you safely inside the shelter, lock the door securely. Snap the padlock, set the dead bolt, and drop the bar into place. Then turn around and walk directly into the dream worlds of Light and Sound.

Protection comes from the ECK Itself.

If you feel the need for extra protection, it is perfectly all right to create several outer chambers inside the entrance. Each chamber is likewise protected by an enormous door; all are safely secured against the night.

Be aware of one thing: The door of protection is made from the ECK Itself. Nothing can get through It!

Journal Your Experience

Write or draw anything you see, feel, hear, or experience during your spiritual exercise.

Journal Your Experience

Write or draw anything you see, feel, hear, or experience during your spiritual exercise.

SOUL TRAVEL

AND DIVINE IMAGINATION

Contemplation Seeds

The imagination is the
God-spark within you.

In the power of divine creativity,
there is no limitation whatsoever.

Soul Travel is an individual
moving closer to the heart of God.

To imagine Soul Travel is the
first thing one must do before
actually getting out of the body.

Love and wonder define
Soul Travel the best.

Create Your Own Soul Travel Adventure

If you are having trouble falling asleep or are afraid, anxious, or excited from your day, use your imagination to create your own Soul Travel experience.

Imagine yourself standing on a beach. Off the shore you see Wah Z approaching you across the water. He might be on a boat or riding the back of a whale or a flying horse. Maybe he is traveling on a cloud. How is he traveling? Look at the details, and describe it to yourself.

Wah Z invites you to join him for a journey across the sea to an island. Hop on! While you travel, look into the water below and up into the sky. What do you see as you make your way toward the island?

Imagine and explore.

When you arrive at the island, Wah Z guides you along a path. What does the path look like? What's it made of—sand, grass, rocks, color, light?

Soon, you reach a fork in the path. Do you turn right or left? What does the path look like now? As the path veers around a corner, you see a shining Golden Wisdom Temple up ahead. What does the Temple look like?

At the door, there is an ECK Master who warmly welcomes you in. What does the ECK Master look like? What are Wah Z and the other Master wearing?

Inside the Temple there is a room just for you. Where is it? How do you get there? You can create this room to look however you'd like. Nothing can enter the room unless it comes with love and you invite it in.

Look around! What do you see?

What colors are the walls?

When you look up, what do you see?

What does the floor look like?

Is there furniture or a fountain?

What sounds do you hear?

Is there another ECK Master there with you?

Do you want to invite any friends or family members to join you?

Enjoy imagining and exploring this room full of love and joy, and remember you can return to it whenever you need or want to.

Whenever you are ready, you can walk back to the shore with the MAHANTA and return home. Or take another journey with Wah Z and see where he takes you next!

A Soul Travel Method

As Soul, we can experience great freedom through Soul Travel. Here is a technique you can try during your spiritual exercises to see all the details of an inner journey.

1. Choose a word to chant, such as *HU, SUGMAD, MAHANTA*, or your own secret word. You can also choose a word from the God Worlds chart on page 117 of this book!

Plan your inner journeys.

2. Close your eyes, and see yourself meeting the MAHANTA. Discuss with him where you would like to go. Do you want to visit a sunny meadow, a beach by the ocean, a mountaintop, or the desert? Or would you like to see a Temple of Golden Wisdom? The choice is yours.
3. Consider how you will travel there. Do you want to take a train, a hot-air balloon, or a spaceship? Or travel on a

cloud? Or will you simply climb a staircase, ride an elevator, or walk along a city street?

4. What would you like to do when you arrive? Are you going to visit a museum, a library, or a planetarium? You can also ask the MAHANTA to show you something new.

Try this exercise several times. Each time, it will be different. Since you are your own travel agent, you can plan your inner journeys any way you want.

Bon voyage!

Dissolving Negative Thoughts

If your imagination picks up harmful pictures or thoughts from somewhere, you can use the following Soul Travel technique to get rid of them.

In your imagination place the image of a golden ECK symbol over the negative thought. Imagine its shining golden light passing through the negative picture. The brilliant light of ECK makes the negative picture fade out completely.

Choose where you put your attention.

You are transforming a harmful aspect of the imagination into a helpful one. This is important to do. The imagination can be your greatest friend or your worst enemy. It all depends on where you put your attention.

How do you want to spend your God energies? It's your choice.

Gateway to an Inner Heaven

When Soul leaves the physical body to journey into the far worlds, It usually goes through the Tisra Til, the Spiritual Eye. There Soul meets the MAHANTA, who escorts It into the heavenly worlds.

Place your attention on your Spiritual Eye.

With your outer eyes open, feel around with your spiritual senses for the location of your Spiritual Eye, the Tisra Til. It can be as simple as placing your attention inside your forehead, between the eyebrows, back an inch or so.

Now close your eyes, and imagine an actual gate to an inner heaven. This is a doorway to God. Give it all your attention as you softly chant *Tisra Til.* Then go through the gateway, and explore what you find there.

In your everyday outer life, you may find yourself more aware of openings—like open doors, windows, or drawers, a break in the clouds, or new opportunities. These signs can remind you of the inner gateway to new spiritual adventures and blessings that the MAHANTA always holds open for you.

Z
Happy Travels

You can use your creative imagination to travel in your Soul body to new places in the inner worlds, just like you go to different places every day in your physical body. The Inner Master is always right there to guide and assist you, if you need him. All you have to do is ask. You can call him by his spiritual name, which is Wah Z or just Z.

Have an inner adventure with Wah Z.

Here are four simple steps to launch you on an inner adventure with him:

1. Sit in a comfortable chair, with your hands resting in your lap.
2. Close your eyes, and look to your Spiritual Eye. It's like the screen of your mind, located behind and between your eyebrows.
3. Relax your physical body by breathing gently three times.
4. Begin to sing the word Z (ZEE). Let the e sound continue. Then sing Z

softly a few more times, either inwardly or aloud.

Keep watching with your Spiritual Eye, and let pictures and colors begin to play across the inner screen. This time picture the color blue, a nice sky blue. Let the blue take any shape it wants, for it is the blue that tells you the MAHANTA is there with you on the inner.

Enjoy seeing the blue light and any other picture your imagination wants to see. Maybe you will picture a tree or a flower. See every part of it. Smell the flower, or touch the tree. Sing Z again. Then speak to the MAHANTA, and tell him you are ready to follow him on a journey. Go with him wherever he leads you.

Try this exercise several times over the next few weeks. Change the color and the pictures you see, but keep using the word Z. Each time, your journey may be different and will give you a new experience of God's love for you.

Happy travels!

The Imaginary Object

Imagination can serve as your inner eyes, just as your physical eyes are your outer eyes.

Would you like to see what Soul can do using the imagination?

Find a place to sit comfortably, breathe deeply, and relax. Place your attention lightly at the Tisra Til or Spiritual Eye, which is just between and behind your eyebrows. If there is anything on your mind, imagine erasing it like you erase a chalkboard until it is blank and clean.

See things from all sides.

Now picture a color. Let the color fill your mind. Let the color change into an object of the same color. Observe this object from above, from each side, from behind, and in front. Now make it shrink—watch it grow smaller and smaller. Make it as small as you can. Now listen. Does the object make a sound? Next, picture yourself doing something with the object. What happens?

* * *

You have just done two important exercises. You've learned how Soul uses the imagination to make pictures and how to see something from all sides. When you want to see the ECK Masters or anything else inside, you can use your imagination, or your inner eyes, in the same way.

Sing *HU* as *H-U*, letter by letter, a few times. Imagine the MAHANTA standing at the bottom of a ladder. Each step of the ladder has the word *ECK* written on it. The MAHANTA invites you to join him on a journey up the ladder.

As you climb, you can see your house, your school, your town, your country, the earth! At the top of the ladder, you land on a soft, puffy cloud. It is firm enough to hold you and the MAHANTA. The MAHANTA takes you on a journey somewhere. It might be to a temple, to another planet, or to someplace very familiar.

Soul Travel with the MAHANTA.

When the journey is over, climb back down the ladder, and thank Wah Z for this opportunity to see your world from a new perspective.

You can use this exercise anytime you need to step back from a situation, explore a new understanding, or travel somewhere new and fun!

Training the Imagination

Your imagination is like a muscle. You can train it every day. What you are actually doing is learning how to become aware and observe yourself in a different state of consciousness.

One way is to go to different places in your imagination. During your contemplation, you can start by re-creating a time spent in nature. Say to yourself, I'm sitting on a big rock or soft ground. What do I see? What plants are around me? What animals do I see? What do the animals look like? What happens when I walk down the path? What is in my backpack? Imagine seeing it all.

Become more aware.

Then, as you go through the day, practice looking at objects and making mental notes. The physical information about the dresser you see or the clothes in your closet will be helpful when you sit down in your chair later and try to visualize those things for a Soul Travel journey in your own room.

Training your imagination is an important first step.

Your Passkey to the Inner Worlds

There is a difference between visualization and imagination. Visualizing means to see pictures in the mind. Imagining is more active: it means putting yourself into the picture and getting involved. The way to put yourself into a picture is through feeling. When you Soul Travel using an imaginative technique, you get involved in what you are visualizing through feeling.

Here are some tips to develop the feeling part of the imagination:

Use all your inner senses.

1. Before you try to Soul Travel, read from the *Letter of Light* or an ECK book. This will stir up your feelings for spiritual adventure and focus your attention on the high reality of the ECK.
2. Listen to music that uplifts you in spirit. For example, an ECK CD or any music that makes you feel good or takes you on an inner journey.

3. Sing *HU* or another ECK word with real feeling, even if you think you don't sing well. Put all your love into singing the word, and let the love return to you as a wave from God. When you feel that wave, imagine and feel yourself riding it. See where it takes you.
4. When you are imagining and creating a Soul Travel experience, use all your inner senses, including seeing, touching, and hearing. Remember that things are much more beautiful on the inner planes than on earth. Don't limit your experiences by expecting them to be the same as on the physical plane.
5. Contemplate on some of the art that appeals to you and gives you a sense of spiritual adventure. Find an ECK picture of a spiritual city, and Soul Travel there to see what it is like.
6. Write down the Soul Travel experiences you would like to have. Include how you would feel and all the details you would notice with your inner senses. After a few months, look over what you have written. You may notice your imagination has started to become more and more real!

Using the element of imagination in Soul Travel is your passkey to the inner worlds!

Journal Your Experience

Write or draw anything you see, feel, hear,
or experience during your spiritual exercise.

Journal Your Experience

Write or draw anything you see, feel, hear, or experience during your spiritual exercise.

Journal Your Experience

Write or draw anything you see, feel, hear, or experience during your spiritual exercise.

THE WONDERS

OF SERVICE TO LIFE

Contemplation Seeds

To be a Coworker means that
no matter what you are doing,
you make it easier
for the next person.

An unselfish dream, goal, or
service can help us to the
height of spiritual living.

When you do something for God,
for the highest principle, you do
each step until it sings.

Take this love I have for you,
and share it gladly with others.
Give it to the world.

Be a Light in This World

This spiritual exercise gives you a way to recognize how you can be a light of love in this world. And it's easy to do!

Close your eyes, and chant *HU*, the love song to God, for several minutes. Then consciously surrender yourself to the love of the MAHANTA. You can even say, "I love you, MAHANTA, ECK, and SUGMAD." Do this in whatever way feels right for you.

Next, gently gaze into your Third Eye, and see the Blue Light of the MAHANTA welcoming you to the inner worlds. Ask him, "How can I be of greater service?" Listen with your heart for the Master's response. You may get a different answer each day.

You are training for Mastership.

Try this exercise for a week or longer. It is a way to learn how to open your heart and serve as a channel for God's love to flow into the world. This is part of your training for Mastership.

A Spiritual-Blessing Technique

Is there a blessing you'd like to receive in your life? It might be for a situation at school, at work, at play, or at home. It could relate just to you, to another person, or even to an animal. Picture the situation clearly in your thoughts, imagination, or feelings, but hold no opinions about the situation.

Next, put the idea or image of the MAHANTA right on top of the situation. Or, if you prefer, you can picture yourself placing the situation directly into the MAHANTA's arms. Know that the MAHANTA's attention is now upon the situation. He will assist in any way possible without interfering with the spiritual lessons of anyone involved.

Now mentally wash your hands of the situation. Let go of it, and say, "May the blessings be." Know that whatever good can come of it, will.

In this exercise you are learning to tune in to the Inner Master, the MAHANTA. You are helping him distribute God's blessings to the world without using your own judgment about what these blessings should be. Because you are not deciding anything on your own, you are being a channel, a vehicle, for the ECK. This means that the ECK is flowing through you the way It wants and needs to. You are not in the way, telling It to do this or that.

Let the ECK flow through you.

Spirit always knows far better than we do what is necessary and best to help each Soul.

Giving Your Gifts

Today, let the Master guide you to give gifts of truth, goodness, love, or beauty to others.

In contemplation, sing *seva* (see-VAH) for several minutes. It is a spiritual word that means a service of love, and it will open your heart to the giving nature of Soul.

Open your heart to the giving nature of Soul.

Declare yourself a vehicle for the Sugmad, the ECK, and the Mahanta. Then imagine the Mahanta walking with you as you go about your day.

At the end of your day, reflect on this exercise. Begin by singing *seva* again. Then inwardly follow the Mahanta's footprints as you retrace your day. Look for the ways the Mahanta helped you give of yourself to others through acts of love and service.

Gratitude as Service

Sincere gratitude is a form of worship.

As you go through your day, consciously look for at least three things you have never expressed gratitude for. Pause and give whatever it is, or whoever it is, your full attention and appreciation.

In so doing, you are accepting more of God's love and being a vehicle for that love to others.

Look for three things you have never expressed gratitude for.

Making Life Easier for Others

Meet every person with the spirit of divine love.

For one day, meet every person that comes your way with the spirit of divine love, and say to yourself, What can I do to make this person's life easier? You may even ask them, "Is there anything I can do for you today?"

See what happens, and write your experiences in your journal at night.

Soul is in this life to learn to give and receive divine love, and Its ultimate goal is to become a Coworker with God. To be a Coworker means that no matter what you are doing, you make it easier for the next person.

Be a Lighthouse to Others

Service to others is a natural outpouring of your love for life and your love for God.

Take a bit of time, and imagine some new ways you'd like to be of service to God in your daily life. This can be at home, at school, at work, at play, or in your community. Make a list here:

Find new ways to be of service.

From the list you made, find ways to volunteer in your community, preferably with other youth. Choose one way, and try it for a day or a weekend. Let the love in your heart shine as a lighthouse to others!

What did you learn about yourself? What spiritual benefits did you receive from giving service to others?

Record your insights in your journal or in the pages at the end of this chapter.

The Golden Pen

The Shariyat-Ki-Sugmad, Book Two, part of the sacred scriptures of Eckankar, says (on pages 200–201), "It is in the small events, such as goodness in the daily things of life, being kind to a child, speaking softly to those who can be hurt easily, noninjury to a fellow creature, and the giving of one's self to others who are without the essentials of life, that spiritual unfoldment can be found."

Today is an opportunity to be a fully conscious channel for the MAHANTA in some natural way that is right for you. What will you do? See how you can serve as a golden heart for God's love today.

Be a fully conscious channel for the MAHANTA.

In contemplation at the end of the day, sing *HU* with all your love. See the MAHANTA bringing you a beautiful notebook and a golden pen. He invites you to record your golden acts of kindness for the day.

Just one act can fill the whole book.

To Be a Greater Flame of Love

The Living ECK Master always brings Light and love into the world. Not just for ECKists, but for every person. This love begins in each of us like a tiny flame, then begins to fill us until we love all because it is life, and life is God's love.

Take a moment to reflect on how your life has improved since you've been practicing the Spiritual Exercises of ECK.

Take a moment to reflect.

Do you have more confidence in your spiritual experiences? More awareness of the things that bring you love and fulfillment?

Close your eyes, and sing *Z*, Sri Harold's spiritual name, twelve times. Ask the Master to show you one thing you can do to become a brighter flame of the Master's love.

The answer may come in this contemplation, in a dream, or in the natural course of your day.

Journal Your Experience

Write or draw anything you see, feel, hear, or experience during your spiritual exercise.

Journal Your Experience

Write or draw anything you see, feel, hear, or experience during your spiritual exercise.

About Sri Harold Klemp

Sri Harold Klemp grew up on a small farm in Wisconsin, USA. Coming from a large family, he faced all the usual challenges of growing up.

His education began in a two-room schoolhouse, and he attended high school at a religious boarding school in Milwaukee. Later, he studied to be a minister, then changed direction and enlisted in the US Air Force. He learned Russian and trained as a language specialist, then as a radio intercept operator.

It was during a two-year term of service in Japan, in the late 1960s, that he first learned about the teachings of Eckankar. He answered an ad in *Fate* magazine which had been placed by Paul Twitchell. That was a momentous occasion! Yet by then Harold had already spent lifetimes preparing for his role as the spiritual leader of Eckankar.

On October 22, 1981, he became the MAHANTA, the Living ECK Master, the latest in an ancient line of ECK Masters who have served as spiritual guides in every age and culture of the world.

Today, Sri Harold loves sharing the ECK teachings with the world. He has a great sense of humor and tells miraculous, true-life stories that help people see the many ways Divine Spirit is at work in their lives.

Above all, he has a passion to show how the Spiritual Exercises of ECK can help us, too, reach Mastership in this lifetime.

To learn more, you might enjoy reading Sri Harold's life story, *Autobiography of a Modern Prophet*. He shares the secrets to spiritual success that he learned on his own journey to Mastership. The spiritual principles and insights he offers can help you find your own path to true happiness, wisdom, and love.

When You Turn Eighteen

A whole new and exciting spiritual adventure awaits you when you step across the threshold to adulthood!

Being an ECK member as an adult gives you the opportunity to advance directly on the path to Self-Realization and God-Realization.

Outwardly, you will receive the adult ECK discourses, which qualify you for further initiation in ECK. Written in a special spiritual rhythm that unlocks the God knowledge already in your heart, these discourses bring an advanced level of spiritual training. They are a living road map to spiritual transformation.

Inwardly, membership is an agreement of the heart between you and the Inner Master, who lights up your dreams and certain events in your daily life as opportunities to practice new spiritual skills and gain higher awareness. It is a rich, very personal, and miraculous adventure that will open you up to new worlds of possibility!

Journey on with the MAHANTA as your inner and outer guide, and go higher, further, and deeper into the worlds of your being! Visit ECKpath.org to learn more.

Books and More

YOUTH ASK A MODERN PROPHET ABOUT LIFE, LOVE, AND GOD

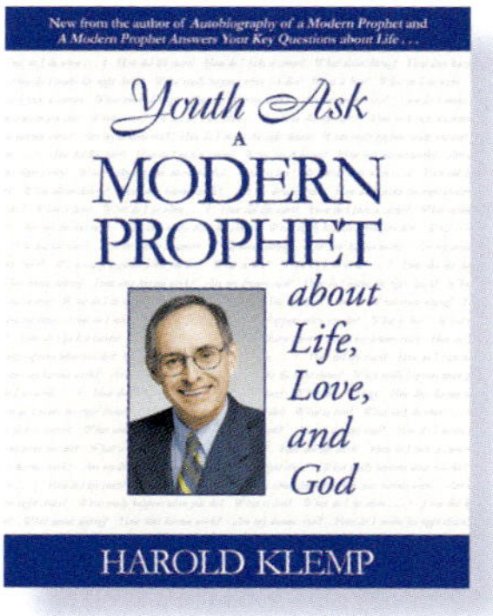

This book is a collection of Sri Harold's answers to the great questions youth from around the world have asked. Their questions range from school challenges, dating, and picking a career to coping with the loss of a loved one, understanding karma, and finding their true spiritual purpose! Often they ask about God, about who we are, and about why we are here. Sri Harold answers every question Soul-to-Soul. His answers may surprise you!

THE ECK RITE OF PASSAGE YOUTH STUDY GUIDE

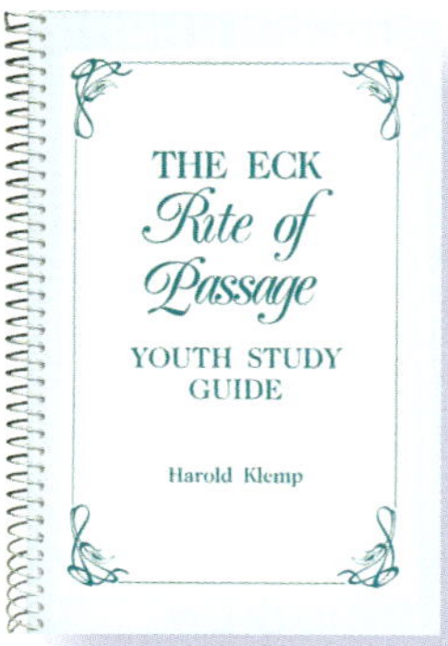

The ECK Rite of Passage celebrates crossing the threshold to adulthood. This special ceremony marks a youth's personal commitment to the ECK teachings and growing awareness of the individual's true spiritual nature.

Each chapter includes an overview of a key spiritual principle of ECK, Sri Harold's answers to related questions, contemplation ideas, and a great spiritual exercise. Also featured are relevant excerpts from Sri Harold's talks, on video and in print.

LETTER OF LIGHT

This colorful, quarterly publication is created by, for, and about youth in Eckankar, the Path of Spiritual Freedom. It expresses the lightness, joy, love, and understanding that come with living the spiritual principles of ECK.

Every issue is filled with creativity, inspiring stories, a spiritual exercise, photos and art, and a very special column where Sri Harold Klemp answers questions from youth around the world. The *Letter of Light* is published, in English and French, in January, April, July, and October. It is sent to all ECK families with children under age eighteen and is also available by annual subscription.

ECKANKAR— ANCIENT WISDOM FOR TODAY

This book presents a wonderful overview of the ECK teachings. You can learn more about karma, reincarnation, seeing an inner light, prophecy, Soul Travel, past lives, and life after death. Discover more about your true identity as Soul, how your dreams can be a source of inner guidance, and how all of these experiences are relevant to your everyday life.

THE TIGER'S FANG GRAPHIC NOVEL

Venture beyond the realms of time and space with Paul Twitchell, modern-day founder of Eckankar, and his spiritual mentor, Rebazar Tarzs. *The Tiger's Fang* is the chronicle of Paul Twitchell's ultimate Soul Travel journey, which can lead you to the heart of God Itself and your own spiritual awakening. Superbly illustrated by former DC Comics artist Mar Amongo.

THOSE WONDERFUL ECK MASTERS

Would you like to have a personal experience with any or all of eleven spiritual Masters? The stories in this book can help you become more aware of the presence and guidance of these amazing Coworkers with God, opening your heart to more divine love, protection, and miracles in your life.

ECK MASTERS AND YOU: AN ILLUSTRATED GUIDE

Filled with extraordinary artwork and renderings of seven ECK Masters and the Golden Wisdom Temples in which they serve, this colorful guidebook opens the door to new vistas of experience for you in contemplation. Prepare for the next step on your spiritual adventure. Your travel guides await you!

Discover more about your true identity as Soul, how your dreams can be a source of inner guidance, and how all of these experiences are relevant to your everyday life.

EXPLORE ECKYOUTH.ORG

This site is a portal for ECK youth around the world to explore and share! Find different ways to get inner guidance. Read the Master's answers to youths' spiritual questions. Learn more about the ECK Rite of Passage. View creative performances and talks by ECK youth. And share your own questions or experiences!

Did You Know?

Here are many of the key terms used in Eckankar. (Words set in SMALL CAPS are defined elsewhere in this glossary.)

Arahata An experienced and qualified teacher of ECKANKAR classes.

Blue Light How the MAHANTA often appears in the inner worlds to the CHELA or seeker.

chela A spiritual student, often a member of ECKANKAR.

ECK The Life Force, Holy Spirit, or Audible Life Current which sustains all life.

Eckankar *EHK-ahn-kahr* The Path of Spiritual Freedom. Also known as the Ancient Science of SOUL TRAVEL. A truly spiritual way of life for the individual in modern times. The teachings provide a framework for anyone to explore their own spiritual experiences. Established by PAUL TWITCHELL, the modern-day founder, in 1965. The word means Coworker with God.

ECK Masters Spiritual Masters who can assist and protect people in their spiritual studies and travels. The ECK Masters are from a long line of God-Realized SOULS who know the responsibility that goes with spiritual freedom.

ECK Rite of Passage One of the Four ECK Celebrations of Life. This ceremony is for youth on the threshold of becoming adults, at about age thirteen. It celebrates a personal commitment to the ECK teachings, to accepting the presence of the MAHANTA, and to becoming more aware of one's true spiritual nature.

Fubbi Quantz The guardian of the SHARIYAT-KI-SUGMAD at the Katsupari Monastery in northern Tibet. He was the MAHANTA, the LIVING ECK MASTER during the time of Buddha, about 500 BC.

God-Realization The state of God Consciousness. Complete and conscious awareness of God.

Gopal Das The guardian of the SHARIYAT-KI-SUGMAD at the Temple of Askleposis on the Astral PLANE. He was the MAHANTA, the LIVING ECK MASTER in Egypt, about 3000 BC.

HU *HYOO* The most ancient, secret name for God. It can be sung as a love song to God aloud or silently to oneself to align with God's love.

initiation Earned by a member of ECKANKAR through spiritual unfoldment and service to God. The initiation is a private ceremony in which the individual is linked to the Sound and Light of God.

Kal Niranjan The Kal; the negative power, also known as Satan or the devil.

Karma, Law of The Law of Cause and Effect, action and reaction, justice, retribution, and reward, which applies to the lower or psychic worlds: the Physical, Astral, Causal, Mental, and Etheric PLANES.

Kata Daki A female ECK MASTER, who, like all others in the Order of the Vairagi, serves the SUGMAD by helping others find the MAHANTA, the LIVING ECK MASTER. Her pet project is to help people get back on their feet during hardship.

Klemp, Harold The present MAHANTA, the LIVING ECK MASTER. SRI Harold Klemp became the MAHANTA, the Living ECK Master in 1981. His spiritual name is WAH Z.

Lai Tsi An ancient Chinese ECK MASTER.

Living ECK Master The spiritual leader of ECKANKAR. He leads SOUL back to God. He teaches in the physical world as the Outer Master, in the dream state as the Dream Master, and in the spiritual worlds as the Inner Master. SRI HAROLD KLEMP became the MAHANTA, the Living ECK Master in 1981.

MAHANTA An expression of the Spirit of God that is always with you. Sometimes seen as a BLUE LIGHT or Blue Star or in the form of the MAHANTA, the LIVING ECK MASTER. The highest state of God Consciousness on earth, only embodied in the Living ECK Master. He is the Living Word.

Mahdis *MAH-dees* The initiate of the Fifth Circle (SOUL PLANE); often used as a generic term for all High Initiates in ECK.

Peddar Zaskq The spiritual name for PAUL TWITCHELL, the modern-day founder of ECKANKAR and the MAHANTA, the LIVING ECK MASTER from 1965 to 1971.

planes Levels of existence, such as the Physical, Astral, Causal, Mental, Etheric, and Soul Planes.

Rami Nuri The guardian of the Shariyat-Ki-Sugmad at the House of Moksha in the city of Retz, Venus. He served as the Mahanta, the Living ECK Master. The letter *M* appears on his forehead.

Rebazar Tarzs A Tibetan ECK Master known as the Torchbearer of Eckankar in the lower worlds.

Satsang A class in which students of ECK discuss a monthly lesson from Eckankar.

Self-Realization Soul recognition. The entering of Soul into the Soul Plane and there beholding Itself as pure Spirit. A state of Seeing, Knowing, and Being.

Shamus-i-Tabriz Guardian of the Shariyat-Ki-Sugmad on the Causal Plane. He was the Mahanta, the Living ECK Master in ancient Persia.

Shariyat-Ki-Sugmad Way of the Eternal; the sacred scriptures of Eckankar. The scriptures are comprised of twelve volumes in the spiritual worlds. The first two were transcribed from the inner planes by Paul Twitchell, modern-day founder of Eckankar.

Soul The True Self, an individual, eternal spark of God. The inner, most sacred part of each person. Soul can see, know, and perceive all things. It is the creative center of Its own world.

Soul Travel The expansion of consciousness. The ability of Soul to transcend the physical body and travel into the spiritual worlds of God. Soul Travel is taught only by the Living ECK Master. It helps people unfold spiritually and can provide proof of the existence of God and life after death.

Sound and Light of ECK The Holy Spirit. The two aspects through which God appears in the lower worlds. People can experience them by looking and listening within themselves and through Soul Travel.

Spiritual Exercises of ECK Daily practices for direct, personal experience with the God Current. Creative techniques using contemplation and the singing of sacred words to bring the higher awareness of Soul into daily life.

Sri A title of spiritual respect, similar to reverend or pastor, used for those who have attained the Kingdom of God. In Eckankar, it is reserved for the Mahanta, the Living ECK Master.

Sugmad *SOOG-mahd* A sacred name for God. It is the source of all life, neither male nor female, the Ocean of Love and Mercy.

Temples of Golden Wisdom Golden Wisdom Temples found on the various planes—from the Physical to the Anami Lok. Chelas of Eckankar visit these temples in the Soul body, under the Mahanta's guidance, to be educated in the divine knowledge. Sections of the Shariyat-Ki-Sugmad, the sacred teachings of ECK, are kept at these temples.

Towart Managi The ECK Master in charge of the Shariyat-Ki-Sugmad in a Temple of Golden Wisdom on the Mental Plane. He was the Mahanta, the Living ECK Master in ancient Abyssinia (now Ethiopia).

Twitchell, Paul An American ECK MASTER who brought the modern teachings of ECKANKAR to the world through his writings and lectures. His spiritual name is PEDDAR ZASKQ.

Vahana The ECK missionary; a carrier of ECK or the message of ECK.

vairag The spiritual virtue of detachment.

Wah Z *WAH zee* The spiritual name of SRI HAROLD KLEMP. It means the secret doctrine. It is his name in the spiritual worlds.

Yaubl Sacabi Guardian of the SHARIYAT-KI-SUGMAD in the spiritual city of Agam Des. He was the MAHANTA, the LIVING ECK MASTER in ancient Greece.

For more explanations of Eckankar terms, see *A Cosmic Sea of Words: The ECKANKAR Lexicon*, by Harold Klemp.